Meaningful
Purpose

Meaningful Purpose

A Primer in Logoteleology

LUIS A. MARRERO
DANIEL E. PERSUITTE

MEANINGFUL PURPOSE
A PRIMER IN LOGOTELEOLOGY

iUniverse books may be ordered through booksellers or by contacting:

iUniverse
1663 Liberty Drive
Bloomington, IN 47403
www.iuniverse.com
844-349-9409

Because of the dynamic nature of the Internet, any web addresses or links contained in this book may have changed since publication and may no longer be valid. The views expressed in this work are solely those of the author and do not necessarily reflect the views of the publisher, and the publisher hereby disclaims any responsibility for them.

Any people depicted in stock imagery provided by Getty Images are models, and such images are being used for illustrative purposes only.
Certain stock imagery © Getty Images.

ISBN: 978-1-6632-3383-7 (sc)
ISBN: 978-1-6632-3213-7 (hc)
ISBN: 978-1-6632-3384-4 (e)

Library of Congress Control Number: 2021925435

Print information available on the last page.

iUniverse rev. date: 05/12/2022

To my wife, Nahir, and our children, Jonathan, Kathleen, Christian, and Christopher. You are all my meaningful, happy thoughts.
Luis A. Marrero

To Isabel, who has been solving life's puzzles since the day she was born, and to Isaac, who is full of love and laughter and seeks to inspire both in others. I could not have asked for two better examples of purpose and meaning.
Daniel E. Persuitte

Contents

List of Illustrations ix

Preface xv

Introduction xix

Chapter 1   What is a Meaning? 1

Chapter 2   What is Meaningful and Important? 42

Chapter 3   The Identity Formula 52

Chapter 4   Motivation 71

Chapter 5   Blocks to Meaning 92

Chapter 6   Meaning of Life and Meaning in Life 103

Chapter 7   The AVR Method 120

Chapter 8   Conclusion 153

Acknowledgments 163

About the Boston Institute for Meaningful Purpose 165

Glossary 167

Index 179

End Notes 189

Bibliography / Suggested Reading 195

List of Illustrations

Figure 1 Meaning-Construct 12

Table 1 Healthy and Unhealthy Meaning Types 26

Table 2 Intelligence and Meaning Types 29

Table 3 Healthy (Strong) and Unhealthy (Weak) meaning-sets................ 30

Figure 2 Meaning Type Intensity Profiles 33

Figure 3 Meaningful / Important Quadrant 47

Table 4 Types of Identities 59

Figure 4 Logoteleology Identity Model 61

Figure 5 The Logoteleology Identity Model in Action (LIMA)................ 63

Figure 6 The Intended-Outcome Model 66

Figure 7 Diagnosing through the Identity Model in Action 67

Figure 8 Motivation = Energy + Direction 72

Figure 10 Energy / Motivational Intensity.. 73

Figure 11 Direction of Motivation 74

Table 5 Types of Motivation... 77

Figure 12 Components of a Meaningful Meaning Ecology..................... 83

Figure 13 Telosponse... 85

Figure 14 The Logoteleology Identity Model in Action (LIMA) 87

Table 6 Meaning Type Congruent and Incongruent Narratives 125

Figure 15 The Logoteleology Identity Model in Action (LIMA) 132

Daniel E. Persuitte, B.A., MLP

Daniel E. Persuitte is a licensed Master Logoteleology Practitioner and a partner in the Boston Institute for Meaningful Purpose. As a long-term student of logoteleology, Daniel has progressed through mentorship with Luis Marrero from pupil to partner and co-author. Working together with Luis to add to concepts, refine theory, and progress models, Daniel also maintains a strong focus on the practical application of meaningful purpose psychology methods and tools.

Daniel has practiced logoteleology throughout his professional roles for more than a decade to significant positive impact and results. As a leader and coach, Daniel has approached life as a living laboratory of sorts, testing MP premises and methods to benefit others and his own perspectives. Consistently receiving feedback from peers and other colleagues that emphasises inspiration, self-awareness, self-motivation and the motivation of others, and a strong focus on the why behind actions and opportunities are examples of how the use of logoteleology has brought positive ends. In addition, Daniel has experienced profound meaning and purpose in his personal life through his journey with logoteleology. He consistently finds meaningful purpose psychology to bring positive outcomes in relationships, planning/goal setting, and achieving meaningful results. This is Daniel's first book, and he plans to continue to write and contribute to the production of materials regarding logoteleology through his continued work in the field.

Daniel is currently a program and team lead in the information technology division at a global insurance and financial services company. Prior to this, Daniel had worked with other highly recognizable brands in the automobile and audio technology industries. In addition to these roles, Daniel has been and remains an active member of several high-profile professional associations and industry groups.

Daniel holds an undergraduate degree in business psychology from the University of Massachusetts—Amherst. Pursuing the education brought a valuable mechanism for growing and evolving his perspectives in all facets of life, among them how to view the way he and others worked in the organizational systems in which they all participated. As meaning, motivation, and purpose were key themes Daniel focused on, progressing through leadership opportunities (both formal and informal) made available chances to put into practice what learnings and other insights he had.

A lifelong learner, Daniel continues his formal education as a current student at the University of Massachusetts Isenberg School, pursuing an MBA specializing in business analysis. Applying this education and the broadening of perspective that accompanies studying, learning, and growing continues to benefit Daniel as a professional and as a student of business, psychology, and throughout life.

Daniel works in Massachusetts, where he lives with his wife Nahir and their two children Isabel and Isaac.

Luis A. Marrero, M.A., RODP, MLP

Luis A. Marrero is the founding partner of the Boston Institute for Meaningful Purpose and the pioneer of meaningful purpose psychology (MP) and Organization Development 2.0 (OD2.0). Since studying and doing his graduate thesis work on Eric Berne's Transactional Analysis (TA) psychology in the late '70s, Luis leveraged his knowledge of psychology, developed methods, and delivered solutions that would meet and exceed business goals. During the '80s, Luis designed 'people-first' leadership and organization development solutions to intrinsically motivate stakeholders to outperform expectations. This 'people-first' approach became the foundation for his OD2.0 theory and methods.

Over time, adding to his TA (influenced by Freud's analytical psychology) knowledge, Luis was later influenced by four masters in their respective fields: Kurt Lewin's social psychology, Viktor Frankl's logotherapy, Alfred Adler's individual psychology, and Harold Bridger's Tavistock. Luis was mentored by Dr. Bridger and taught Tavistock laboratories at NTL Institute during the '80s and '90s. These giants of the field, in addition to others, helped him shape the propositions to what is today meaningful purpose psychology, or its scientific name, logoteleology, the subject of this his second book.

While his interventions were successful, Luis was intrigued by what social, economic, and organizational macro-indicators revealed. Psychology and other solutions were having a limited positive impact in people's daily lives and within organizations. Instead, these indicators were going in the wrong direction over the years; discovering why this phenomenon was happening and finding a remedy became a life quest. This quest led to the creation of meaningful purpose psychology and his first book, The Path to a Meaningful Purpose: *Psychological Foundations of Logoteleology.*

Even before the publication of The Path, Luis has been applying, refining, and teaching logoteleological methods and solutions to therapists, consultants, counselors, coaches, college professors, industry leaders, and the general public. In addition, through his practice as a coach, OD consultant, and assessing leaders, Luis, with fellow collaborator, Daniel E. Persuitte, has been polishing both the theory and approaches. This second book reveals the theory's advancement.

Luis earned his B.A. in History from Siena Heights University in Adrian, Michigan, and his M.A. in Human Resource Management from the University of Puerto Rico. In addition, he did post-graduate studies at NTL Institute, The Academy of Modern Applied Psychology and earned professional certifications. He conducts psychological and leadership assessments, coaches, and consults with Fortune 500 companies worldwide.

Luis lives and works in Massachusetts and Florida with his wife, Nahir. He enjoys riding his bicycle and studying psychology, leadership, and history.

Preface

Meaningful purpose psychology—or its scientific name—*logoteleology,* is the study of the meanings that enable individuals and communities to thrive. The name logoteleology is derived from the Greek "Logos," "Thelos," and "Telos," terms that translate to "substance or meaning," "will," and "purpose," respectively. The more common name of meaningful purpose psychology, and the oft-used shorthand MP, appear throughout this text but are used interchangeably with the logoteleology term.

Meaningful purpose psychology (MP) is an optimistic and positive science that describes how people and organizations give meaning to the self, others, and situations; and how such meanings can and do lead to a consequence. It is optimistic and positive because it posits that problems can be prevented and many times resolved in meaningful ways. Moreover, MP can solve individual, interpersonal, group, organizational, and even national challenges.

Throughout the coming chapters of this text, the concept of *meaning* will be discussed at length, including definition, foundations, implications, understanding, etc. For now, think of *meaning* as the opinion, view, interpretation, assumption, hunch, feeling, mindset, and even belief about yourself, other people, and situations you encounter in your daily life. Once we have meanings, they guide us to engage in ways compatible with that opinion or worldview.

> Ex. Say, for instance, that I have a great person for a leader. Because I believe her to be such a wonderful person, no one would be surprised if I spent time eagerly learning from and seeking her direction.

As we know, meanings lead to consequences. In this case, the results of my high-esteemed meaning could be varied. For instance, I might seek some of my leader's positivity and competence to rub off on me. In many ways, I like how she leads, and I would like to lead similarly. If her leadership can make me feel good about myself, I can do the same for others. In other words, she is a model worth emulating. This sort of reverence (meaning) may lead me to be hopeful (consequence) about the benefits of her leadership. Further yet, the simple advantage of feeling good about myself may be in and of itself something that I wish to continue to experience, and that too is a consequence of what my leader's leadership means to me.

From a different perspective, a consequence could have to do with her authority to delegate to, coach, and develop me. I can learn from her and perform interesting work to advance my career. Here, the potential consequence is professional advancement.

Consider a third consequence or outcome of my supervisor being such a great leader. When others ask me about my experience working for her, I would be very much inclined to praise her talents and style. This praise, in turn, enhances her reputation within the organization, increasing the odds that *she could be promoted* sometime in the future. Hence, besides opportunities for professional advancement, some additional favorable consequences for my leader would be having others' esteem and respect.

I am sure you can draw cause-and-effect examples from your own life experiences to explain how a meaning leads to a consequence. Understanding this causal relationship is at the heart of MP. While a logical and straightforward concept, leveraging this understanding for the person, group, organizational, and social benefit has eluded the many to our detriment. Hence, the paradox.

The Paradox

Logoteleology came to be the result of an ironic paradox. Why are we inundated with knowledge accessible through simple internet searches, higher learning institutions, libraries and bookstores, professional journals and books brimming with best practices, gurus, coaching, training, and consulting organizations, and yet, we are over our heads with intractable human-made problems? Or as stated in The Path to a Meaningful Purpose: *Psychological Foundations of Logoteleology*

> *Mankind…does not suffer from a lack of answers. Rather, it suffers despite the answers being available.*

Logoteleologists know why this paradox is detrimental, and we are optimistically ready to help others escape from its clutches to experience life to its fullest. This Primer will provide the fundamental tools to understand and apply meaningful purpose psychology to your benefit, as well as for the well-being of those you relate with daily. The knowledge and insight gained from this Primer on your path to a meaningful purpose can equip you to become the leader, partner, parent, student, friend, mentor, professional, and person you wish to be.

We wish you all the best on your journey.

Luis A. Marrero
Daniel E. Persuitte
October 2021
Meaningful Purpose: A Primer in Logoteleology

Introduction

The following text was written as a collaboration between the two managing partners of the Boston Institute for Meaningful Purpose. Over the last ten years, Daniel E. Persuitte and Luis A. Marrero have been working with MP in different ways. Luis has been teaching and practicing as a consultant and coach, working with individuals and client companies both domestically and internationally. Daniel has been applying and exploring the concepts and methods while working in business leadership positions in the technology, insurance, and financial services industries. The breadth of this experience is brought to bear throughout this book to enhance the applicability and usefulness of the material. We strongly believe that this diversity has led to a strengthening of the science and a more engaging reading experience.

One of the most common questions we get when discussing logoteleology, also referred to as meaningful purpose psychology, or commonly just MP, is "who is it for?" Reflexively we can start to explain how MP can bring benefit to people. After all, it has application in professional settings, interpersonal relationships, social clubs and organizations, therapy and coaching, and much more. Yet the true answer to the question "who is it for" is even more straightforward than that…

It's for us

We all walk a path in life, and while the stops along that path can be important milestones that are formative to so many, there is meaning too in the steps between those milestones. We use the phrasing "it's for us" here with a sort of dual meaning. It is for "us" as in each of us as individuals, but just as important, it is for the collective "us" who interact with each other in different ways and in different contexts throughout life. In addition to meaningful purpose psychology helping us understand our own meanings, it helps us learn both to ensure those meanings are being conveyed to others as truly intended and to interpret the meanings others communicate. When we communicate meanings accurately, we reduce or eliminate misunderstanding, negative attributions, and other problems big and small that often happen when we miss the meaning mark. Ultimately, in addition to conveying meanings, the goal is to convey healthy, uplifting, and edifying meanings.

What makes up meaning and how meaning leads to purpose is at the core of MP. The term "meaning" is defined and discussed in detail at the start of *Chapter One: What is a Meaning,* but for now, we'll say that a meaning is an expression, impression, or intent backed by reasons, motives, and justifications; and purpose is the translation of meaning into a plan of action, in other words, the carrying out of a meaning.

Throughout this text, these concepts of meaning and purpose will be broken down to show how they are at play in all parts of life, beginning with factors that shape our meanings from birth up through the way that we interact with others in our day-to-day activities. In fact, that you're reading this book right now is influenced by some meaning or meanings that translated to purposeful action. When we understand what is behind how the circumstances and situations of life are experienced, we can decide for ourselves, or help others, to modify, change, and recalibrate to carry out the meaningful purpose each of us has.

> *Do my actions support what I want to happen in my life?*
> *Do I know what the meaning of my life is and why that matters?*
> *Am I personally connected to my life goals?*

These are just some examples of questions that will be addressed in ourselves or in those we counsel by using the information, concepts, and tools contained in the chapters that follow. Using MP, we can realize benefits such as

- Identifying the meaning of life for each of us
- Understanding what we strive for as human beings
- Recognizing how our own identities lead to the way we take in, interpret, and convey information

- Determining what in life we deem to be meaningful and important, and taking care not to misplace importance on what is meaningless
- Enriching the steps on our paths with meaning, purpose, and the motivation we use to get where we truly want to go in life

When we first started writing this book, it was going to be a field guide, but as the work came together, it made more sense as something foundational with practical elements. Thus, we chose to explore the core elements of MP, add examples for clarity and understanding, and provide reflection questions and exercises for each chapter's material. The text that follows was written with the hope that it would be accessible to practitioners of meaningful purpose psychology and those who will use the understanding and application of these methods and concepts for the benefit of others through therapy and counseling, leadership, coaching, and other support services. It is also intended for individuals who seek to learn and apply MP on their own personal and interpersonal journeys.

The seminal text on logoteleology, or meaningful purpose psychology, is *The Path to a Meaningful Purpose* by Luis A. Marrero, one of the coauthors of this book. While The Path introduces the core components of MP, the information contained throughout this book updates, clarifies, breaks down, and simplifies concepts while adding more examples that will help recognize them in the context of relatable life experiences. We have also added a summary and review section, along with reflection questions at the end of each chapter, which reinforce the content of each section and invite additional viewing angles and ways to think about the material. Finally, there are sections titled "Apply MP!" at several points throughout this text, which take material that has been introduced and provide a way to think about its practical application. The inclusion of these elements helps understanding and application and creates a foundation upon which to build.

The material starts with the definition and structure of what makes a meaning and ends with the practical application of MP through our AVR method©. The AVR method© is the proprietary MP framework for meaning analysis and improvement. As we engage in the introduction of logoteleology (MP), we establish the basic terms and concepts so that we can build on these throughout the text. Following the initial definition of meaning and why meaning is important, we break down the six elements that make a meaning.

These are called meaning types, or MTs. They are Attributes, Beliefs, Values, Feelings, Attitudes, and Aims.

These MTs contribute, and even interact, to produce meaning-sets that can be *internally focused* as part of who each of us is; our unique Identity Meaning DNA Set (IMDS), or *externally focused* such as in the Situational Meaning-set (SMS). These elements of meaningful purpose psychology provide a strong base upon which we'll continue to build our understanding of how meaning-sets shape our worldviews. Additionally, how they influence the way we interact with others and our ability to break down and adjust any flawed or otherwise unhealthy MTs.

Continuing to build upon the structure in place from the first chapter, we'll discuss in *Chapter Two: What is Meaningful and Important* how some meanings can be given prominence in focus or significance and how they may not be aligned with our goals in life. We'll also learn about The Five Meaningful Life Strivings (Love, Peace, Happiness, Engagement, and Prosperity) and how they represent what we as humans yearn for throughout life in different ways. Love, for example, is an easy enough concept to grasp as it relates to romantic, friend, or family relationships. Still, it could be more challenging to understand how this applies to a typical professional or organizational setting. Love can be understood as acceptance, respect, appreciation, recognition, and a feeling of being valued and valuing others. The Five Strivings are necessary elements of experiencing meaningfulness. When any of these is absent, we should look to our underlying meanings and seize the opportunity for improvement.

Pursuing the Five Strivings in a social context means interacting with others. We introduce the ACT (Allow, Cooperate, Transcend) framework as a way to guide us as we seek to promote meaningfulness in these circumstances for others and ourselves. We all have a right to our individuality and the pursuit of what we want to achieve. It is up to us to allow each other that pursuit, to aid one another in what ways we can, and by doing so achieve more meaningful benefits than if we had chosen to proceed in a self-focused and solitary manner.

We'll end the second chapter with a deeper dive into what makes a meaning important, unimportant, meaningful, and meaningless. This section is critical to understanding what happens when we place importance on meaningful things instead of what is meaningless. We'll define and contrast "meaningless" as insignificant and lacking purpose or value. We'll also show how people can often give significance to meaningless things in their lives and perspectives. Understanding this is a significant step toward making the changes needed to redirect the prominence away from these and toward more meaningful focuses.

In *Chapter Three: The Identity Formula*, we explore what makes us each uniquely identifiable as people, members of a group, and specific roles we perform. These identities that we have carry meanings as well, and they can strongly influence how we see the world around us and ourselves. Throughout the chapter, we learn how identities are formed, such as through cultural or family upbringing, socioeconomic factors, or education, and how they influence what each of us determines to be meaningful. In addition, identities have meanings that determine how we act and interact throughout our lives. To illustrate and better understand this relationship between identity and meaning, we introduce the Logoteleology Identity Model or LIM. The LIM is a formula that breaks down how meanings with motivation and purposeful action equal an identity. In other words, how someone would see themselves in a role (a parent, for example) is made up of what meaning they give to that role, how strongly they feel about it, and how they act on that meaning and motivation.

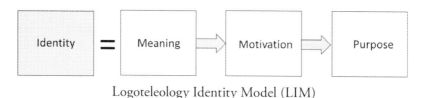

Logoteleology Identity Model (LIM)

A person in college might say that "Having grown up in a family that placed a high value on education, and being a student currently, I actively push myself to study hard." A lot is happening in this short statement. From it, we can glean that there are at least two identities at play here, one is a student, and another is a member of a family. We can also see from the statement's content that these are both important to this person, which speaks to motivation. Let's take another look at the statement through the lens of the LIM:

"Having grown up **in a family** (identity) that placed a **high value on education** (meaning), and being a **student** (identity) currently, I **actively push myself** (motivation) to **study hard** (purpose)."

The LIM helps us comprehend the meaning, motivation, and purpose that are related to identity. This understanding is very valuable when finding purpose in what we do, boosting motivation that may be lacking, and connecting to meaning that might not be obviously apparent.

Building off the LIM, we finish the third chapter by introducing the LIMA, or Logoteleology Identity Model in Action. This model adds three more elements, which are contact, consequence, and feedback.

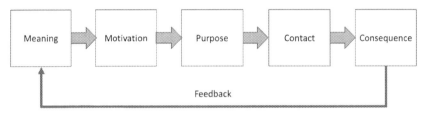

Logoteleology Identity Model in Action

The LIMA is to be used to understand interpersonal exchanges, impacts, and consequences. For instance, as a member of a family that places high value on education from the previous example, our student might add to their statement that they feel proud when their family members recognize their academic achievement. By using the LIMA, we understand the family members represent the contact because they are the other side of this interpersonal interaction. We also see a consequence in that the student experiences a feeling of pride, which is meaningful to them, as a result of the actions in which they engaged. This feedback lets the student know whether or not their meanings have been fulfilled. In this case, the feedback reinforces their meanings. If the feedback does not support the meaning, this is an indication that there is an accuracy problem. Determining the source of the problem and coming up with potential adjustments is needed to find the solution that will improve the outcomes and the feedback.

Motivation plays a big part in both the LIM and the LIMA, but in *Chapter Four: Motivation,* we dive deeper into the role of motivation in MP more broadly. After defining motivation as energy plus direction, we dive into detail the ways motivation is produced by the strength of meanings and translates to purpose.

$$Motivation = Energy + Direction$$

There are different levels of motivation that this chapter explores.

1. When engaging in activity that is not supported by strong meanings, energy may be low
2. If the activity is carrying out strong meanings, then the energy level may be high
3. If the activity produces outcomes that oppose a strong meaning, the energy may also be high, yet the direction of that energy is away from the activity

These three examples show us that it is not enough to think about motivation in terms of the energy level, as in high motivation or low motivation. We must also think about it in terms of directionality. We may feel strongly about something and highly motivated, but that could just as easily manifest in opposition as it could in support.

We dive into the factors that make up our meanings and how they form a meaning of life in chapters five and six, respectively. Discussing how biogenetic factors, family, culture, learned lessons and experiences, and our own current situations determine meanings and context shows how each of us uses these influences to establish and live with our worldviews. These antecedents provide a strong connection to what is meaningful in our lives, or when the meanings are unhealthy, form blocks to meanings that need to be overcome. When these blocks happen, there are ways to recognize and replace those unhealthy meanings with healthy ones.

What is the meaning of life?

It's a big question, one that's been asked by many to be sure. It's also one that each of us has an answer for—if we know how to look for it. *Chapter Six: Meaning of Life and Meaning in Life* defines and differentiates these two concepts and explores how each of us has an operating meaning of life, whether we are aware of it or not. For many, the meaning of life is default or predetermined by some preselected life script, the expectations of some role, person, or social identity, or a predestined worldview and mission. When we have a prescribed understanding of the world and our place in it that came from outside of ourselves, we have a default meaning of life.

The other meaning of life choice is self-determined. Unlike the default meaning of life, this option involves freely choosing our own identity and mission in life. The text will take you, the reader, through the steps of becoming aware of which meaning of life you use. This awareness comes from analyzing quality, determining if any changes are needed, replacing a default with a self-determined operating meaning of life, building upon the new foundation, refining it over time, and sustaining it going forward. We all can choose the meaning of our lives if we understand where they come from, how we operate within them, and the impact this operation has on our life's outcomes.

In contrast to meaning *of* life, which is about identities and carrying out a mission, meaning *in* life, on the other hand, has to do with what each of us finds motivating and gratifying. While the basic concept of what each of us considers meaningful in life is simple enough to understand, meaning in life can be at times very complex. People can lose sight of what is meaningful to them or find meaning in meaningless things or activities, such as engaging in destructive behavior to themselves or others. Purposefully identifying what is meaningful in our lives allows for something to connect to and determine if our actions support or run contrary to those meanings.

The AVR method© chapter (Chapter Seven) will be especially beneficial for practitioners working with MP. The chapter will cover all seven elements of the method (meaning awareness, analysis, validation, re-decision, replacement or realignment, and reintegration) in detail, providing examples as well. Included at the end of the chapter is also a case study taken from a real MP coaching interaction.

By examining the different types of meanings, we come to a more robust understanding of why we experience things as we do. This understanding also allows us to effect change in our current lives and choose the path ahead of each of us more purposefully. Whether your intent is self-development, working with others, or both, it is our sincere hope and belief that the concepts and methods contained in this text will provide the tools needed to support your meaningful purpose.

The material of MP is so broadly applicable that it is encouraged that you connect personally by finding and considering examples in your own everyday life to go along with those provided in this text. Doing so will help you make a very beneficial personal connection to the elements of MP as you further develop your meaningful purpose lens, noticing more and more that they are a constant as each of us lives out our meanings.

As we practice MP as a way of life, the effects can be felt. They are experienced through how we see the world and the place each of us has in it.

Meaningfully,
Dan & Luis

Chapter One

What is a Meaning?

Meanings set the agenda and guarantee and explain the outcome.

Logoteleology Axiom

After reading this chapter, you will be able to…

- Define meaning and its building blocks
- Understand the different types of (situational, identity, transactional, and transformational), and distinguish healthy from unhealthy meaning-sets
- Explain why meanings, meaning-constructs, and meaning-sets are relevant

Can you recall situations where you wonder, "why is this happening?" feeling confused, resentful, or in pain? Or bewildered, you think to yourself, "this doesn't make any sense." Yet, there might be other situations where things flow smoothly and without difficulty. Is there a way to confidently understand outcomes and the reasons behind our general state of happiness and success? If so, how can understanding meaning and its role in personality help us know what is *really* happening and keep us grounded in reality? Meaningful purpose psychology's (MP) definitions and explanations of meaning help people be more self-aware and discerning, leading to more apparent perspectives. Understanding meaning empowers us to shape the way we experience our lives and the world around us. Consequently, we can confidently select choices that promise the most beneficial results.

This chapter is the longest of the book, and for a good reason. The content of Chapter one—meaning—is the cornerstone of meaningful purpose psychology theory. The content of this chapter is meant to be read in various sittings, allowing time for study and reflection, appreciating the implications of all the parts, making connections, seeing the whole picture, and finding ways to apply them in your life and practice.

What is a Meaning?

Viktor Frankl, a professor and scientist who devoted his life's work to meaning-based psychology, provided a straightforward answer: *"Meaning is what is meant,* be it by a person who asks me a question, or by a situation which, too, implies a question and calls for an answer." [ii] Additionally, "There is only one meaning to each situation, and this is its true meaning." [iii] These statements from Frankl tell us that every situation and action has a question element, and the answer to the question is the meaning.

Here are two additional and complementary definitions of "meaning" from the Merriam-Webster Dictionary: [iv]

- The idea that a person wants to express by using words, signs, etc.
- Something meant or intended

To Mean, What is Meant, and To Aim

These definitions complement Frankl's in that meaning performs two tasks in communication:

1. *To convey the context of the meaning.* This first task must express meaning to another, as in "this is what I mean." This expression is integral for the process of forming conclusions, judgments, or inferences. Parallel terms for *"what is meant"* include a narrative story, motive, reason, basis, and action justification.
2. *To convey an aim through an intention* or a goal. An aim can be either an intention ("this is what I want to do about it") or a goal ("this is what I will do about it."). An uncertain aim reveals an intention. On the other hand, a goal is a confident and specific aim.

Intentions communicate our hopes, dreams, wishes, and options. They come to us as unfulfilled possibilities, choices, and preferences. To intend means we are not ready to commit; instead, we are deliberating. When we intend, we can waver in uncertainty, fluctuating among and weighing options. We grasp for more information, undecided, hanging in suspense to find the correct answer. For instance, think of times when you have wanted to improve in any area of your life and yet, were held back from acting because you were not ready to commit. The point is that "I intend to…" does not mean, "I will…"

Synonyms for *intending* include resolve, disposition, volition, and determination, which "all refer to a wish that one means to carry out." [1]

Remember that an aim-goal is a confident commitment worth investing in because it leads to action and achieves the desired result.

"Meanings are interpretations, the sense you make of your current circumstances. Whether you acknowledge it or not, you forge meanings all day long."

~ Barbara L. Frederickson ~ [2]

Effective communication transmits meaning, whether verbal or non-verbal, which can be thought of as an exchange. A conversation with another person, for example, is a meaning exchange that can be analyzed.

Ex. Think of a mother on a phone call with her son who recently left to start his university studies. The mother may ask the son questions about adjusting, making it to his classes on time, and enough. She may ask how he is getting along with his classmates and whether he's made friends.

We could infer that the mother's *aim* for questioning is to make sure he is okay, that she wants him to have a successful adjustment at the university, and to communicate she loves him. If the son decodes his mother's concerns as caring, we could conclude that communication was helpful because there is a shared and complementary understanding of both reasons and aims. He could presume, "She is calling (aim) because she cares for my well-being" (reasons or justification).

Key Learning Points

Meaning performs two tasks:

1. Justify (What is meant)
2. Aim (What is intended or committed through a goal)

Meaning is a singular aim backed by reasons, motives, and justifications.

Human conflicts, intractable problems, and many mental disturbances derive from flawed motives, reasons, or justifications.

Meaning:

- is information
- has consequences
- holds the content of our identity and outlook of life.

Each person has their unique meaning DNA. It defines who they are (i.e., reasons or justification), and what is their life aim (i.e., intentionality). There is a reason for one's existence and an aim or mission to fulfill.

Consequences reveal and explain the meaning and quality of our lives; what we aim for, be it positive and meaningful or negative and meaningless or portions of both. We all have a default meaning DNA, and consequence explains its meaning aim.

However, what if the son interprets the conversation differently from what the mother meant, perhaps thinking that his mother does not trust him or believe he can handle his independence and studies? If this were the case, the son would have his own set of explanations to contradict his mother's. If the reasons don't match, communication is ineffective, and there would not be a shared meaning. He could think or say, "She is checking on me (aim) because she does not trust me to handle myself" (reasons or justification).

Meaning performs two tasks: (1) justify in order to (2) aim.

Meaning is a singular aim backed by reasons, motives, and justifications.

Misunderstanding creates a disconnect with the "true meaning" referenced by Frankl. Dictionary.com defines misunderstanding as a "failure to understand correctly; mistake as to meaning or intent." [3] Assuming conflict between mother and son, they will need to determine which version of the reasons stated are correct. Misunderstandings are common and have various degrees of gravity. That explains why mix-ups are studied and treated by many professionals—including Logoteleologists—to minimize their occurrences in daily life.

Human conflicts, intractable problems, and many mental disturbances
derive from flawed motives, reasons, or justifications.

Agreed meanings are a pre-condition to getting on with the task at hand. Ideally, when communicating with another, the message should be sent and received as meant and intended to ensure both parties remain "on the same page." The communication must be valid, honest, and transparent, or free from petty gamesmanship. The exchange of practical, trustworthy, and complementary meanings can create a space called *cooperation*.

Again, productive meaning exchanges (i.e., communication) should be genuine and apparent. We propose people should—if they wish to live a meaningful life—avoid wasting time and other resources through

- Real or contrived ignorance

- Unscrupulous tactics (such as avoidance, selective listening, and passive-aggressive behavior)
- Deliberate misinterpretation of reasons and aims

Instead, we should all strive to

- Acknowledge ignorance, be willing to learn, and seek correct information
- Be truthful and transparent by saying what we mean and meaning what we say
- Inquire about hearing and understanding what was meant, and the meaning of what was said

From Meaning to Consequence

Meaningful purpose psychology (MP) practitioners give importance to meanings' *reasons* and *aims* because they have consequences. The influence of meanings transcends the casual everyday exchange of information. Meanings can be a force for good and evil, peace or war, prosperity or poverty, happiness, or a depressive state.

Take a closer look at one of the two tasks of *meaning* as "something meant or aimed." Consider the Merriam-Webster dictionary's definition of [to] "mean": [vi]

- To have in mind as a purpose: intend
- To serve or intend to convey, show, or indicate: signify
- To have importance to the degree of
- To direct to a particular individual
- To have an intended purpose

The Free Dictionary defines [to] mean as

- Something that is conveyed or intended, especially by language, sense of significance
- Full of meaning, expressive [4]

In MP, we use these definitions of "meaning" and "to mean" to explain how individuals aim (intend and set goals), convey and grant significance and priority. For instance, if someone thinks highly of and respects another (reasons), the odds are high that the receiver of such admiration will be treated accordingly—with deference, kindness, and courtesy (aim). On the other hand, if the other party is perceived as rude and self-centered (reasons), we might not be surprised if others do their best to avoid them (aim).

Hence, meanings have consequences.

Apply MP!

Use this learning to comprehend the reasons, motives, and justifications for how you feel about what you do professionally. This understanding will explain your level of engagement and satisfaction. The content of your meanings determines the goals you set for your work. A person experiencing the "Monday blues" or who celebrates "hump day" on Wednesdays or "finally Friday" at the end of the workweek is expressing meaning dissatisfaction with their work experience. When we start the week with worthless meaning content, the experience is as well. The meaning content needs to improve for the experience to improve. Better meanings equal better experiences.

Meanings as Psychological DNA

Meanings also hold the content of our identity and outlook on life. Each human being has a unique psychological meaning DNA that

- Defines who they are
- Justifies why we live (for what cause or mission)
- Aims to fulfill a mission

A person's reasons and aims (i.e., meanings) determine the meaning of life.

We believe that individuals who are fully aware and have vetted, validated, and committed to their meaning of life, stand a better chance of thriving than those who have not.

*"We are **self-determined** by the meaning we give to our experiences, and there is probably something of a mistake always involved when we take particular experiences as the basis for our future life. Meanings are not determined by situations, but we determine ourselves by the meanings we give to situations."*

~ Alfred Adler ~ [5]

All Humans Have a Default Meaning of Life

We believe there is no such thing as a person lacking meaning in life. Even when ignorant of the drives that influence life choices, a *default meaning of life* is in control. An unexamined default meaning of life can negatively affect the quality of life due to aimlessness or misdirection.

Have you ever wondered why habits that don't serve you well are so difficult to change? Think of a challenge that has proven difficult for you to overcome. It could include trials such as losing weight, quitting smoking, managing your finances, or your inability to stop being overly critical of yourself and others. What role could your meaning of life play in improvement prevention?

What decisive role have your meanings and meaning of life played in overcoming challenges through an optimistic lens? The good news is that a determined and well-managed meaning of life can be a *true north* to a thriving life.

There is a reason for one's existence and an aim or mission to fulfill.

Chapter Six will cover the topics of the meaning of life and meaning in life in greater depth.

Key Learning Points

Meaning DNA hold each person's "meaning of life." There are six meaning types:

1. Attributions: What opinion do I have of myself?
2. Beliefs: What are my assumptions? How much do I know?
3. Values: What code of ethics guides me?
4. Feelings: How do I feel about this situation? What is my intuition sensing?
5. Attitudes: How likely am I to do this?
6. Aims: What will I do?

Meaning types organize into meaning-sets. There are two types of meaning-set:

1. Situational Meaning-set
2. Identity Meaning DNA Set

Meaning-set explains behavior and is formed by five meaning antecedents:

1. Our biogenetic DNA
2. Family (psychosocial) influence
3. Culture (socio-cultural) or following dominant social norms
4. Accumulated learning and life experiences (biographic history)
5. Current situation and context

Meaning Type analysis is a gate to self-regulation and winning in life.

Why are Meanings Relevant?

So far, we've explored what meanings and psychological meaning-DNA are, as well as their consequences. In this section, we will explain the relevance of meanings.

Meanings

- Are communicated
    - The quality of communication determines the likelihood of cooperation
    - When meaning is shared and mutually understood, an agreement is very likely
- Fulfill two tasks
    - Provide reasons
    - Convey aims
        - Aims and their supporting justifications can be positive and meaningful or negative and meaningless
        - We have free will and the power to select our reasons and intentions, or goals
- Are fulfilled by a construct of six factors or types related to reasons, motives, justifications, and aims (intentions and goals)
    - Factors for reasons, motives, and justifications are
        - Attributions
        - Beliefs
        - Values
        - Feelings
        - Attitudes
    - And for intentions and goals, the factor is
        - Aims
- Determine and explain human behavior
    - We can assess what our reaction says about our meanings and intentionally and thoughtfully select meanings and compatible actions to thrive in life
- Carry consequences
    - The quality of the meaning determines the potential quality and impact on others
    - Meaningful reasons can produce significant outcomes

- Hold the content of our life's DNA (e.g., identity and meaning of life)
  - Discovering the content of your meaning-of-life-DNA can allow you to appreciate the quality of your life and to select those meanings that will serve you and others best

"Meaning comes from commitments that transcend personal interests; it comes, as Frankl put it, from 'reaching out beyond the self toward causes to serve or people to love.'"

~ Joseph B. Fabry ~ [6]

What are Meanings Made of?

We explained that meanings accomplish two tasks

1. Provide justifications (what is meant)
2. Determine an intention or a goal (what is the aim)

These two tasks are achieved through a *meaning-construct* composed of six *meaning types (MTs)*. The term *type* signifies that each carries information and has a unique role and agenda to fulfill within the meaning-construct. When these six MTs interact, they are called a *meaning-set*. The function of the meaning-set in human conduct serves as a processing mechanism, taking in information and determining how to respond, adapt, and thrive in its environment. The meaning-set is critical in determining the category and level of motivation and purposeful action.

What is the Difference Between Meaning-construct and Meaning-set?

The *meaning-construct* is a theoretical model that contains, defines, and explains the dynamics of six MTs. This model is critical to understand, develop, and determine meaning. How those elements act (and interact) to form a person's meaning is called the *meaning-set*.

Consider the example of a trip to a doctor's office to treat a stomach ulcer. In the office, the doctor has an anatomical model of the human digestive system. This model is similar to the *meaning-construct* in that it is systemic or made up of parts working together. Using the model, the doctor may point expressly to where you, as the patient, are experiencing the problem. In this way, the doctor's narrative of the patient's symptoms is like the *meaning-set* in that it's referring to something specific going on in one of the system's parts.

Using an example from a psychology perspective can help to illustrate further what happens with the meaning-construct and meaning-set. Mental health practitioners may use psychometric tests built using a theory and a model. Once a report is generated, the findings provide data about the client analyzed against the factors. The meaning-construct is like these factors in that it allows for data on the MTs that are at play. The meaning-set, as an analysis of those factors, can be thought of like the resulting report.

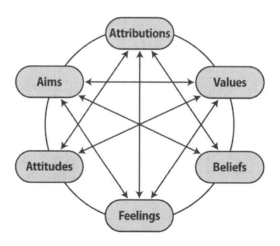

Figure 1 Meaning-Construct

The six meaning types are:

1. **Attributes**: A person's defining and inherent character traits or qualities; an ascription or designation of intent. These two elements of the attributes meaning type can be further explained as

    a. the definitions we use to describe others and ourselves. For instance, a person could have intelligence or morality as attributes

12

b. intent placed onto others and ourselves. People attribute intent when they impute actions or consequences. Attributes include natural inclinations, strengths, and talents. For example, "He loves working with people" is attribution in that we infer the subject's love for working with people through observing actions, expressions, etc.

This meaning type holds the individual's self-image and the image attached to others. Also, the attribution meaning type explains our self-esteem and the esteem we have toward others. Attributes' dark side ascribes malicious and insensitive intents and characterizations against self and others. If asked to describe yourself or to describe another, Attributes are where you would likely begin. The Attributes meaning type answers the sample question, "Who am I?"

"If we close our ears to words and concentrate on observing actions, we would find that each person has formulated his own individual 'meaning of life,' and that all his opinions, attitudes, movements, expressions, mannerisms, ambitions, habits, and character traits are in according to this meaning."

- Alfred Adler - [7]

2. **Beliefs**: Is a firmly held opinion or conviction, a view of what is true or real. Beliefs can also include assumptions, truisms, suppositions, points of view, opinions, and perspectives. What we would refer to as common or general knowledge, as in being able to recognize and describe a chair or knowing that harming another is wrong, are beliefs. The source of Beliefs is knowledge. We all carry a mental video library, dictionary, and encyclopedia in our Beliefs meaning type. Hence, *Beliefs receive, hold, and recall information,* including the life experiences and other memories that inform and shape them. The Beliefs meaning type is the intellectual information bank.

The source of Belief is knowledge.

Humans can sometimes hold beliefs without proof, that is to say, believing in something in the absence of firm evidence or conviction. Belief without *evidence* is referred to using words such as "faith" or "delusion." On the other hand, the presence of doubt reduces or prevents certainty (*conviction*), weakening the Belief meaning type (MT). It can be said that knowledge becomes belief when the person accepts it with conviction. This acceptance happens regardless of the actual veracity of the information. The Beliefs MT also has a dark side, such as when it holds biased information, withholds the truth, resists new information, fabricates alternate realities, or lies. We protect against this dark side through a robust Value MT placing importance on honesty and integrity.

A task of life is to prove beliefs grounded on substantiated or concrete evidence. Beliefs answer the sample question, "What assumptions am I making about this situation?"

"...people develop beliefs that organize their world and give meaning to their experiences. These beliefs may be called 'meaning systems,' and different people create different meaning systems." "...people's beliefs about themselves (their self-theories) can create different psychological worlds, leading them to think, feel, and act differently in identical situations."

~ Carol S. Dweck ~ [8]

3. **Values**: The Values meaning type reveals a person's principles or standards of behavior. These principles are used to judge and determine what is proper and vital when making decisions. It also includes commitments and promises made. For example, committing to be at a specific place at a determined time and upholding that commitment could be an example of an operating value. Examples of Values include ethics, moral code, right/wrong, correct/incorrect, acting with integrity, and righteousness. *The values meaning type is the depository of the human conscience* and is tasked with regulating behavior. Values' dark side is the lack of guiding principles and conscience. Values answer the sample question, "What ethical code regulates my decision-making?"

"Values, defined by Frankl as 'universal meaning,' under normal circumstances provide useful guidelines toward meaning." [9]

"Nevit Sanford pointed out that educators must do more than emphasize values. They must stress the meanings behind values." [10]

~ Joseph B. Fabry ~

"Logotherapy conceives of conscience as a prompter which, if need be, indicates the direction in which we have to move in a given life situation. In order to carry out such a task, conscience must apply a measuring stick to the situation one is confronted with, and this situation has to be evaluated in the light of a set of criteria, in light of a hierarchy of values." [11]

"In view of the possibility of finding meaning in suffering, life's meaning is an unconditional one, at least potentially. That unconditional meaning, however, is paralleled by the unconditional value of each and every person." [12]

~ Victor Frankl ~

"Modern life offers people a wealth of some forms of meaning, but it doesn't offer clear guidance about fundamental values. The 'value gap,' as I shall call it, is the single biggest problem for the modern Western individual in making a life meaningful."

~ Roy F. Baumeister ~ [13]

4. **Feelings**: The Feelings meaning type is a sensory, affective, and intuitive experience. Feelings mean something. They help answer the question, "What is behind this sensation?" We use our senses of smell, touch, taste, hearing, and sight to interpret and describe people, things, and situations. Feelings help us explain an event's affective experience, for instance, love, peace, serenity, fear, anger, pain, joy, inspiration, and exhilaration. When we crave, yearn, relish, long for, and desire, we are feeling. Finally, feelings also include intuition. Intuition reveals itself as a hunch, perception, and instinct. Feelings have a dark side, including examples such as depression, despair, and hate.

Feelings do not come from nowhere; feelings mean something.

In MP, feelings are not the same as emotions (i.e., energy in motion). To feel is an intrapsychic event, while emotion is energy invested to fuel interaction with a target within the environment or outside oneself. Remember that meanings convey content, context, and aims, not action. Feelings operate within meaning-sets, and emotions work outside the meaning-set. Hence, emotions are not part of a meaning-construct. Instead, as will be explained later, emotions are part of the motivation-construct.

"Labeling of a sensation is one way to define 'meaning.'"

~ Sonia March Nevis ~ [14]

5. **Attitudes**: the learned, relatively stable tendency to respond to people, concepts, objects, and events in an evaluative way through a like/don't like continuum. For instance, some people have a positive attitude toward playing with children, while others have a negative attitude toward eating frog legs.

   Feelings incite attitudes. This cause and effect relationship is shown in our attitudes toward someone or something affected by feelings of love or disgust. Imagine a person's attitude, brought about by these intense feelings, and how they may behave differently depending on it. In this way, attitudes betray/reveal temperament and disposition. Influenced by other MTs, Attitude's darker side is to avoid people and situations without a valid motive. The Attitude meaning type answers the sample question, "How likely am I to follow that path?"

"Meanings in activities and experiences are easily perceived. More difficult to see is Frankl's contention that meaning can also be found in attitudes when we face unavoidable suffering."

~ Joseph B. Fabry ~ [15]

6. **Aims**: The Aims meaning type is either an *aspirational striving* (need or desire) or a *compulsory drive*. Aims explain what the person intends to do or become. The distinction between aspirational or compulsory aims is determined by the situational context and the quality of the

meaning-set content. For instance, concerning the quality of the content, a meaning-set can have either healthy or faulty MTs.

A dominant feeling type that conveys compassion, supported by a constructive disposition (i.e., attitude) to serve others, is an example of a healthy meaning type. As a rule, a healthy meaning type has an intrinsic or willing disposition and is most likely aspirational.

On the other hand, faulty (dark side) MTs could lack ethical values for effective self-regulation and a misinformed belief system prone to errors. There are times when the reasons within faulty MTs produce a driven or compulsory (kneejerk) aim. When people state, "I don't know why I reacted that way!" they betray a faulty compulsory meaning-set. There are other times when ignorant or disagreeing MTs (e.g., cognitive dissonance) cause inaction. For instance, when we say, "My heart tells me to stay, but my mind tells me our relationship will not work."

As a rule, an aspirational aim willingly strives and yearns for something virtuous worth accomplishing. It is generally well thought out and intentional, but it is not always the case. As we know, the quality of the MT determines the ultimate result. People can have the best of intentions and still not be able to achieve their goals.

On the other hand, a compulsory aim feels reactive, coercive, forced, and imposed. As a rule, aspirations are intrinsic (they come from within), while compulsory drives are extrinsic (originating externally).

Finally, Aim serves as a critical thinking gate where meaning content is vetted. An effective Aim meaning type gathers and consolidates all the available data and ensures congruence between all MTs. Without this alignment, MTs cannot lead to effective action. Incongruent or misaligned information as determined by the Aim meaning type is often experienced as procrastination, reckless, compulsive, or reflexive behavior. The Aim processes data from all MTs and controls meaning outputs. It makes sense of all information to ensure there is a clear and considered cause before proceeding. For example, in a problem-solving business meeting, the facilitator will usually review and make sense of all the relevant information to justify action. Another way to think about it is that the Aim meaning type acts as a Central Processing Unit (CPU) controlled by operators (e.g., If-then).

Apply MP!

We feel things all day long. Understanding the MTs that trigger feelings (Feeling is a meaning type) allows you to identify what you are sensing and what caused the sensation. For example, when someone is experiencing fear, what they think (Belief meaning type) they are afraid of is often not the actual trigger. Instead, the meaning the person gives to the situation is the true source. It isn't the roller coaster ride that we fear, for example. The fear we experience comes from the belief in the potential consequence of getting on the ride (e.g., the fall). Understand the MTs and how they work to determine what drives the avoidance (Attitude meaning type).

Aim-Intent and Aim-Goal

Beyond aspirational and compulsory, the Aims MT needs to be understood in terms of strength and resolve. As previously referenced in the definition of meaning, Aims have two types, aim-intent, and aim-goal.

The first, aim-intent, is characterized by a directional uncertainty or a weakness in resolve. An example of aim-intent might be a person desiring to participate in the Boston Marathon yet lacking a plan to make that participation a reality. Another good place to look for aim-intent examples is on bucket lists (the things we'd like to do before we "kick the bucket"). These are commonly aspirational without necessarily having any definite plan to achieve them.

The second type, aim-goal, is distinguished from aim-intent due to the strength of direction and resolve, "I will compete in the marathon this year," for example. The aim-goal type is confident and committed to achieving the target intention.

The Aims meaning type is last because the first five provide motives (*what is meant—reasons and justifications*). Still, Aims conclude and determine intent and goals depending on the particular aim type's strength and resolve. Terms strongly related to the Aims meaning type include conclusion, completion, decision point, and resolve. Finally, aims answer the sample question, "What do I intend to do?"

"Man is not fully conditioned and determined but rather determines himself whether he gives in to conditions or stands up to them. In other words, man is ultimately self-determining. Man does not simply exist but always decides what his existence will be, what he will become in the next moment."

~ Viktor Frankl ~ [16]

The Dynamic Nature of Meaning-sets

MTs interact, collect and process data (e.g., make sense) and decide what to do (i.e., Aims). As previously stated, when MTs interact as a collective, they are defined as a *meaning-set.*

"One scientifically tested way to stop this life-draining cycle is to dispute negative thinking. Dispute it the way a good lawyer would, by determining the facts. Let me go back to my own downward spiral. What set it off? What negative thoughts and beliefs got triggered? What did those thoughts and beliefs in turn make me feel? And how those thoughts and beliefs compare to reality? What are the facts of my situation? When I take in those facts—truly take them in—how do I feel?"

~ Barbara L. Frederickson ~ [17]

A Meaning-set in Action

Let's explore a meaning-set in action through the lens of a fictitious university student, Mary.

Mary sees her professor at a distance and remembers she owes him a class paper, which she has not written. She would be embarrassed to face him; so, she ducks into the nearest store to avoid him.

Seeing the professor at a distance, Mary

1. determines the professor could/would reprimand her (*Beliefs* meaning type)
2. knows she is not meeting her *standards* (*Values* meaning type) of what a responsible person does
3. labels herself as careless and negligent (*Attributes* meaning type)
4. feels embarrassed and mortified (*Feelings* meaning type) of confronting her professor
5. spurs an *attitude* (*Attitudes* meaning type) of avoidance at all cost
6. *decides* to hide from the professor (*Aims* meaning type)

In the linear form, Mary's meaning-set mental process would look like this:

Beliefs → Values → Attributes → Feelings → Attitudes → Aims

However, the meaning-set's cognitive processes can be (and are) more complex than the simple illustration above. These processes happen quickly, and most of the content of this type of dynamic progression is subconscious. However, it serves to illustrate the point.

Apply MP!

Meaning-constructs give us the confidence to understand what is going on inside of us and in our surroundings. A company's rewards program, for example, conveys its values (meaning type) and expectations. Remember that a company's policies, operating procedures, and norms are all examples of where we would see their values on display. However, values in an organization may be misaligned, which can result in conflict. For instance, the sales division finds value in the close of the sale, while the finance department finds value in the receipt of the payment. The reason for the difference comes from the objective of each area's work focus. The sales department's work culminates with the deal, but finance does not see their work complete until the payment is collected. To eliminate the conflict, ensure there is meaning alignment for both parties (e.g., shared values in the form of metrics, norms, or policies). Through this example, we have shown how meanings precede behaviors using the values meaning type. However, any of the other MTs can have this same logic applied. For instance, conflict can lead to unfair attributions, negative attitudes, and hostile feelings toward other parties.

The Transactional and Transformational Meaning-set

Meanings exchange or transact information internally within the set and with the external environment. The exchanged information is meant to meet the daily needs and wants of life's demands and satisfy innate aspirations to improve and thrive, transcend, and find meaning in life.

Examples of *internal transacting meanings* to satisfy our daily needs and wants include deciding what dress or suit to wear for work or visiting your place of worship, pondering how to best tackle a problem, and contemplating what could have brought on a headache. They can also include wanting to satisfy a thirst when dehydrated or to sit on a comfortable sofa to watch a movie. Think of *internal transacting meanings* as self-talk.

Examples of *external transacting meanings* include aiming to ask another person what time it is, intending to order a meal at a restaurant, and planning to pay a supermarket cashier for articles purchased. It is important to note that these transacting meanings are related to the Aims meaning type and are not actions. The Aim meaning-type content will be used to determine whether there is action to follow and what that will be. More on this when we discuss motivation in Chapter Four. External transacting meanings also include an exchange of acknowledgment and affection or asking questions. These meanings always point directionally toward interaction with something or someone outside of us.

Transactional meanings have a dark side. A flawed internal transacting meaning can be excessively self-serving, for instance, in the case of hoarding and obsessive-compulsive (OCD) disorders. These can also be overly confident (i.e., overconfidence bias) and narcissistic.

Meaning exchanges can also be transformational. Here the goal is to go beyond daily life transactions. A *transformational meaning* desires a meaningful life—to thrive and succeed. A transformational meaning can be *self-oriented* or *other-oriented*.

Key Learning Points

Meanings exchange or transact information within the set (i.e., internal), and with the external environment. The exchanged information is meant to meet the daily needs and wants life demands, and to satisfy innate aspirations to improve and thrive, to transcend and find meaning in life.

- Internal transacting meanings is self-talk.
- External transacting meanings entails engaging in the outside environment

Transformational meanings seek to thrive and succeed.

- Self-oriented transformational meanings want to grow and to be validated by others.
- Other-oriented transformational meanings support others' needs and want to improve.

People operate within a meaning exchange economy to meet needs. These exchanges can be reciprocal, freely given, conditionally given, or one-sided. When meanings exchanges are proportional, relationships are bound to flourish. Disproportional meanings are experienced as unfair and stressful.

Meaning-sets can be consonant or dissonant. Self-determined consonant meaning-sets produce meaningful information, feelings, and aims. Dissonant meanings have faulty content that creates discord.

A self-oriented transformational meaning seeks self-development and validation from the external environment. Attention is primarily in meeting the self's innate needs, wants, and goals. An example of a *self-oriented transformational meaning* includes engaging in activities compatible with becoming an authority in a field, such as studying, gaining experience, and engaging with prominent experts. You may be involved in *self-oriented transformational meaning* at this very moment by reading this book.

Other-oriented transformational meanings support others' development and improvement. Attention is primarily intended to meet the needs, wants, and goals of others. Examples of *other-oriented transformational meaning* include financially sponsoring an orphan's education, providing career coaching to a junior employee, and mentoring the underprivileged. The goal of the *other-oriented transformational meaning* is to edify others.

Meaning Exchange Economies

All humans need stimulus, recognition, and care. These are expressed through needs, wants, and goals. To meet these desires, people interact with others. As discussed, attention can be focused on the self or others. Meanings can be given and withheld. Given meanings can be reciprocal (i.e., quid pro quo) or selfless. Hence, people exchange meanings to meet their goals. Meanings are withheld to communicate apathy, disdain, reprove, or to practice prudence in some circumstances.

The quality of relationships depends on how just and equitable the exchange of meaningful meanings is.[18] David G. Myers (2005) defines equity as "A condition in which the outcomes people receive from a relationship are proportional to what they contribute to it." But, he adds, "Equitable outcomes needn't always be equal outcomes." [19] Consistent with equity theory, the MP Method is in the *meaning currency business* seeking to help people understand the relationship between transactional and transformational meanings and their quality of life.[20]

Each meaning type has something meaningful to give and a need to fill. For instance:

- *Attributes (and attributions)* provide a positive appraisal of others and expect others to reciprocate

- *Beliefs* share information with others and yearn to learn
- *Values* establish rules and principles to get along and want others to state the standing norms and conditions to relate well
- *Feelings* trigger nurturing emotions and need to receive in turn
- *Attitudes* show approval and expect inclusion by others
- *Aims* reach out to others and expect constructive feedback to improve

Meaning exchange economies also have a dark side. They can be intended to use, misuse, and abuse others through deprivation, manipulation, and other selfish and harmful aims.

When meaning exchanges are proportional, relationships are bound to flourish. Conversely, disproportional exchanges of meanings are experienced as unfair and stressful. Logoteleologists work to create and foster meaningful economies, leading to individuals' improved ability to bring about the positive results they seek.

What Determines the Health of a Meaning-set?

A healthy meaning-set has meaningful content, and the MTs are in accord. Using the term "healthy" signifies that the meaning is loving, promotes peace and happiness, engages in activities that add value, and brings prosperity to all stakeholders. In this way, the meaningful edifies, builds, is ethical, and brings the best out of oneself and others. A healthy meaning-set is discerning and wise. Conversely, when the meaning-set's content or reasons are unhealthy and flawed, the aim can be expected to be equally prone to produce mistakes or errors of judgment. These errors end up harming the self and others in some way. Hence, meaning-sets can be consonant or dissonant. Consonant meaning-sets render meaningful information, feelings, and aims. Dissonant meanings have faulty content that creates discord.

Consider the example of Thomas, a supervisor of a manufacturing facility. Thomas constantly threatens and reprimands his employees when their work does not meet his standards of perfection. Rather than helping them overcome their weaknesses, he tells them "try harder," which has a discouraging effect on his staff. Thomas's leadership style fits the definition of a meaningless or unhealthy meaning-set.

Meaning Types	A Healthy Meaning Type	An Unhealthy Meaning Type
Attributions	Exhibits self-confident, growth-minded, and prosocial behaviors. Highlighting and encouraging others' potential for good. Genuinely strengthens others' self-esteem and capacity to succeed. Is guided by a self-determined, clear, and confident meaning of life determined to contribute. Is open to feedback to improve oneself.	Exhibits awkwardness, fixed mindset, and antisocial behaviors. Demeans and discourages others. Chooses to harm oneself and others. Operates without awareness of any meaning of life and is fraudulent or misinformed. Is closed to feedback and unwilling to acknowledge error and fault. May suffer from imposter syndrome.
Beliefs	Has a correct understanding of the nature of humans and what is possible. Is based on knowledge because it is empirical, which leads to sound judgment and wise decision-making. When taking positions, individuals are careful and realistic, not misrepresenting evidence, but acknowledging their limits and ignorance. Is grounded in evidence and veracity. Constant learner and seeker of truth. Unbiased. Is willing to go against the crowd when impartial evidence proves doing so is apt.	Has a diminished and incorrect understanding or estimation of humans and their potential. Is opinionated and lacking knowledge. Lacks critical thinking skills to help make informed decisions based on truth. Is stubborn and inflexible when presented with contrarian fact-based evidence. Subscribes to herd mentality (groupthink) and is unwilling or incapable to think independently due to peer pressure and low self-esteem or self-confidence.
Values	Brings and lives by humane standards. Has a clear, proven, confident, prosocial, and determined code of ethics that does well for oneself and others. Subscribes to and follows morals. Knows what is essential and attends to priorities. Acts with integrity and righteousness in all their dealings. Committed to allowing others to be themselves, cooperate, and transcend to practice altruistic principles. Respects and promotes good manners, etiquette, decorum protocols, accommodative policies and procedures, and regulations of civility. Committed to win-win outcomes. Capable of self-regulation. Operates from a vigorous conscience. Is trustworthy and dependable.	Lacks a clear, proven, confident, prosocial, and determined code of ethics. Does not seek or prioritize mutual benefit in interactions or dealings. Compromises to meet ends even when damaging to other stakeholders. Is devious, spiteful, erratic, and lacking consistency when making judgments and decisions, consistent with Machiavellian and narcissistic personalities. Is uncultured, without good taste, manners. Lacks decorum and displays a defiant disposition to social norms. Unable to self-regulate. Has a diminished conscience and is untrustworthy.

Feelings	Are loving, caring, respectful, empathic, sensible, peaceful, enthusiastic, optimistic, and self-assured. Displays a positive, happy, and genial mood.	Is insecure and uncomfortable with oneself and others. Has difficulty expressing optimism and exchanging affection and is perceived by others as lacking enthusiasm and empathy. Display depressive, pessimistic, uncertain, and angry moods.
Attitudes	Inclusive, other-oriented, and outgoing. Has an upbeat and "can-do" disposition toward life. Is attracted to socialization with others and welcomes inclusion. Possesses a positive outlook on life, people, and situations (healthy attitudes are the same as positive attitudes.)	Is unfairly or unwisely exclusive and selective of company. Tends to be socially indifferent and disinterested (may be described as a loner.) Wavering when unsure, and tending to either avoid conflict and be timid or be overaggressive and forthright when stressed. Possesses an ultimate goal of avoidance; either by removal from the presence of others or pushing others away in some manner. Holds a negative view of life, people, and situations (unhealthy attitudes are the same as negative attitudes.)
Aims	Includes and displays the previous MTs' healthy dispositions: has noble attributions, is knowledgeable and truthful, acts with integrity, and reveals virtuous feelings and attitudes.	Includes and displays the previous MTs' harmful temperaments: possesses low self-esteem and negative attributions, is ignorant, is corrupt in dealings, holds onto negativity in emotions and outlooks, and pushes away and avoids others.

Table 1 Healthy and Unhealthy Meaning Types

Logoteleologists, or practitioners of meaningful purpose psychology, help people discover what makes a meaning healthy and follow an edifying process for human-thriving through self-determined ways.

What Determines the Intelligence of a Meaning-set?

We learned that meanings could be healthy or unhealthy. Meanings can also be intelligent or unintelligent. Intelligence "can be described as the ability to perceive or infer information, and to retain knowledge to be applied towards adaptive behaviors within an environment or context." [21] Intelligent meanings are empirically well-informed and aligned with objective reality.

Below is a table with intelligent and unintelligent descriptions and examples of MTs.

Meaning Type	Intelligent Meanings Are	Unintelligent Meanings Are
Attribute[22]	Knowledgeable of human's capacity to adapt to the environment. Aware and understanding of the self and have realistic expectations based on strengths and weaknesses. Striving to become one's best self. Possessing a growth mindset.[23] • The certainty of one's potential. "I have the potential for doing good." • Taking responsibility for what is within one's locus of control.	Influenced by a demanding Values meaning type, having unrealistic and unfair expectations. Unaware or unknowing of the self. Unable to leverage strengths and improve on weaknesses. Possessive of a fixed mindset.[24] • Low self-esteem or impostor syndrome. "I am worthless and a fake." • Deflecting responsibility when bad things happen.

Belief	Basing decisions and choices on factual and evidence-based or empirical information. Using truth and reality as a foundation for subsequent actions. • Testing the soundness of a vaccine through rigorous testing before immunizing the public.	Basing decisions and choices on opinion, hearsay or gossip, blind faith, following unhealthy traditions and norms, and ignorance. Alternatives do not pass the truth and reality test. • Operating under the belief that some ethnic groups are superior to others.
Value	Virtuous. Proving and being convinced of the value of following win-win norms and standards that benefit and uplift all concerned. Having a clear ethical and moral code to influence decision-making and choice. • Returning a found wallet full of money to its owner.	Lacking an empirically proven and well-thought-out set of norms to self-regulate to success. Disconnected and unaware of standards when making choices and decisions. • Cheating on one's tax returns.
Feeling	Positive, genuine state of well-being and mood that brings one's and others' best. Aware of sensations and their meanings; responding appropriately. • Becoming aware of a headache and considering what caused it to apply the correct remedy.	In a poor state of well-being; lacking joy, a peaceful mind, or mindfulness. Not in tune or fully experiencing sensory inputs. Underperforming intuition and having blind spots that prevent clear sensory perception and impact on the self and others. • Unable to show empathy when another loses a close relative.

Attitude	Remaining self-aware of dispositions and their meanings. Attracted to pursuing noble gratifying goals and avoiding postures that detract from meaningful success. Showcasing in oneself, and inviting in others. • Displaying a confident "can-do" and tempered disposition under challenging situations.	Unaware and out-of-touch with one's mindsets and their consequence. Having negative pessimistic dispositions when facing challenges. Distancing and dodging tendencies. • Having a glass "half empty" and avoidant outlook. Playing it safe to prevent embarrassment through failure.
Aim	Goals that can respond well to environmental demands and meeting personal needs and wants. Selecting goals that bring the best in oneself and others. Leading to genuine prosperity. Following a thoughtful, thorough and systematic approach. • Determining to learn about an unknown but essential subject.	Missing the mark. Pursuing goals destined to fail and that prevent enjoying life to its fullest. Unable to meet personal and environmental expectations. Lacking critical thinking skills. • Deciding to act without evaluating or the right skills to succeed.

Table 2 Intelligence and Meaning Types

Strong and Self-Determined Meaning-sets

A robust meaning-set is healthy and intelligent. It makes well-informed decisions that benefit all concerned. A meaning-set that is healthy and intelligent has harmonious and congruent meaning types (MTs). Healthy and intelligent meanings are the foundation of wisdom, and hence of a life worth living. Wise and healthful meanings are self-determined and therefore strong and confident.

A self-determined and strong meaning-set has valuable content and effective processes that produce worthwhile outputs. Illustrated in the table below, we can see how this flow happens. Each part of the pattern has meaning intelligence and health. For example, a vigorous meaning-set holds accurate and abundant (content) information in each meaning type, and its functions are harmonious and synergistic (process). As a result, they produce excellent and meaningful judgments (output).

Meaning-set	Characteristic	Strong Meaning-set	Weak Meaning-set
Content	• Amount • Quality	• Abundant • Excellence and Empirical	• Scarce • Poor and Theoretical
Process	• Meaning Type • Harmony and Cooperation • Synergy	• Stable and Congruent • High (1+1=3)	• Unstable and Incongruent • Low (1+?=?)
Output	• Intelligence • Impact	• Good Judgment • Meaningful	• Poor Judgment • Meaningless

Table 3 Healthy (Strong) and Unhealthy (Weak) meaning-sets

Understanding that a robust meaning-set's content has considerable and trustworthy information is just half the story. On the other hand, when the content is weak, it betrays a scarcity of reliable and truthful information. The meaning-set is robust when all MTs are engaged, agreed, and capable of creating synergy when processing data. Conversely, a weak meaning-set cannot create synergy because the MTs do not cooperate reasonably. Meaning-set outputs are strong when they have truthful and complete information to make wise decisions that benefit all concerned. In contrast, a weak meaning-set's outcomes are unable to produce effective and valuable choices.

Apply MP!

As intelligence in meanings improves, so does the health of the meaning outcomes. Think of how many times throughout any given day we make decisions to carry out meanings—meanings that have to do with how we approach situations, treat other people, or our wellness. A healthy meaning builds up; it is mutually beneficial and is positive. If what we do conflicts with the healthy outcome, there is potentially missing or erroneous information at play. Find the knowledge needed to improve meaning intelligence and boost health. The more we exercise this, the more it becomes a habit. The habit shapes due to the effect that improved intelligence has on developing and strengthening our conscience. A strong conscience guides us toward healthy outcomes.

Situational Meaning-sets and Identity Meaning DNA Sets

Another way of understanding and studying meanings is by observing how they respond to the context or environmental demands.

Logoteleologists carry out meaning-set analysis to help people understand their motives and aims, as in Mary and her professor's case. People experience these types of *situational* or *transactional meanings* hundreds, if not thousands of times each day. Moreover, situational meaning-sets respond to environmental demands, just as in the earlier example where we saw the way Mary's meanings reacted when she saw her professor.

Sometimes meanings are aligned with others', and sometimes they are not. *For example, group, or team, meaning alignment,* indicates harmony and agreement among members. As a result, the group's task can continue its course. Conversely, *group meaning misalignment* demonstrates that the members are not in sync. An example of a misaligned group at the meaning level is apparent when there is a lack of role clarity, not knowing who will do what and when. These misunderstandings and incongruences are commonplace and can result in the need for apologies, explanations, restatements, and sometimes (if not handled well) leave a rift between parties involved. Therefore, it is crucial to understand what meanings are and their role in behavior for these and other reasons. Specifically, it is essential to be mindful of potential consequences when attributing meanings to self, others, and circumstances.

For further reading and supporting documentation, we encourage reviewing the theories of Richard Beckhard and separately Jack Gibb (specifically the helpful Gibb's model). References are included in the bibliography for specific suggested articles. [25]

There are two types of meaning-sets:

1. A *Situational Meaning-set* is a momentary, narrative, sensory-filled, and affective collection of organized MTs primed and intended to respond to environmental demands. Together, these MTs process information (i.e., think, reason, justify) and make decisions (i.e., decide, adjudicate, aim). For example, the analysis of Mary's thought process earlier in this chapter illustrates a situational meaning-set.

   People thrive, relate, adapt, and strive to cope in their surroundings through situational moment-to-moment meaning transactions. Because each situation is unique, the meaning type content and ultimate response will remain adaptable and harmonious with situational or contextual demands. Consider, for instance, that if Mary, from our earlier example, had seen her loving boyfriend at a distance instead of the professor, her response (meaning-set content and dynamics) would have very likely been different. Thus, again, Situational Meaning-sets are transient, dynamic, and adaptive based on context. This transitional state is consistent with the self-directed or logoteleological nature of humans, where meanings determine action.[26]

   Roles and context can also determine which MTs will play an active and prominent part. For instance, a judge's ruling in a court could have his Values meaning type play a dominant role in managing process and judgment while keeping his Feelings and Attitudes MTs at bay to prevent giving an impression of being biased. In turn, a clinician with a distressed client could have a more active Beliefs meaning type to understand symptoms and an empathic and intuitive Feelings meaning type to discern and encourage while holding back on judging (Values meaning type) and attributing intent.

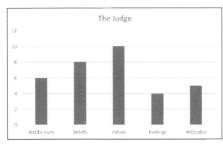 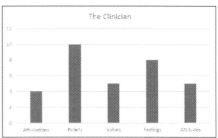

Figure 2 Meaning Type Intensity Profiles

2. The second type of meaning-set includes the previously introduced *meanings as psychological DNA* or an *Identity Meaning DNA Set (IMDS)*. IMDS is a collection of organized meanings that highlight the uniqueness of a person's identity. The IMDS carries the psychological individuality and imprint of each human being. Because of the unique IMDS, no human being is the same and cannot be replaced by another.

    Also, the IMDS set is more stable and constant, and as the name suggests, is based on a sense of self. The IMDS determines our worldview. As a rule, Situational Meaning-sets will generate aims or intents consistent with the IMDS.

Why is the difference between Situational and Identity Meaning-sets relevant?

Situational Meaning-sets (SMS) relate to behavior as the IMDS refers to an identity. The IMDS has to do with *who I am* and the SMS with *how I behave*. For example, in Mary's case, there is a difference between acknowledging she had not done her homework (how Mary *behaved*) and attributing she *is,* as part of her identity (who Mary *is*), irresponsible. Not being able to distinguish between behavior and identity can lead to mental disturbances. Persistent negative attributions in a meaning-set will incite agreement on damaging behavior (self-fulfilling prophecy) at the IMDS. If Mary incorporates into her IMDS that she is irresponsible, her SMS will likely behave accordingly.

In logoteleology, mental disturbance is the outcome of meaning-set dissonance.

Instead, to pursue a healthy IMDS, Mary could acknowledge she did not act consistently with her values. She would also assume responsibility and commit to correct her course. Her goal would be to act or behave consistently with who she is or aspires to be, as in "I am a responsible person."

Appy MP!

All of how we think about and respond to things in life involves meaning. The situational meaning-set (SMS) is at play when we frame circumstances in relation to ourselves in the context, as in how equipped we are to handle a task. On the other hand, the identity meaning DNA set (IMDS) operates when we frame circumstances in relation to the context and ourselves, as in how I am as a person makes me equipped (or unequipped) to handle a task. For example, this function may show when a person needs to accomplish a job but is frustrated because they lack the skills and training. The SMS may tell them that they don't have the skills to succeed, but the IMDS might lead them to believe they aren't good or smart enough. This same contrast is possible in whatever context you experience in your own life. If you conclude that the problem is a lack of skills, the solution can be to obtain the necessary training to get them. However, if you make a negative or unfair attribution about yourself (or another), you may end up framing it as an unsolvable problem. The negative attribution is understood as fixed, which may lead to seeing the root cause (lack of knowledge) as paralyzing. You can quickly gain the information needed, but changing who you are is a far more complicated, possibly insurmountable problem.

As an example, say that you aspire to a job that requires a college degree. Using the IMDS, you might tell yourself that you aren't the kind of person who goes to college. This lack of confidence can make it impossible for you to get the role. However, if you think about it using the SMS, you may determine that you need to go to college to get the degree necessary to get the role. This example illustrates the difference between the situational approach versus the potentially incapacitating way of viewing the challenge through the IMDS.

For further helpful reading, we encourage you to review the work of Carol Dweck, specifically the growth and fixed mindsets. [27]

Meaning Antecedents

As mentioned previously, in addition to these dynamic SMS's, each person has an individual *meaning imprint* or *meaning DNA* (IMDS) that sets them apart from others. The uniqueness of the IMDS has a profound influence on life. Remember, Viktor Frankl defined meaning as *"what is meant"* and Merriam-Webster as *"what is meant or intended."* So, we could ask, *"what is the meaning of my life"* and *"what do I intend to do with it?"* The answer is psychologically imprinted in everyone's unique identity. Frankl's definition of meaning implies that each human being has a default meaning of life—a meaning of life that, ideally, can evolve, grow, and improve through uplifting edification. But, on the other hand, it is also possible that such meaning of life can be corrupted to harm self and others (i.e., psychopathic conditions).

This meaning of life is a mission determined by what we call *meaning antecedents*.

There are five *meaning antecedents*:

1. Our biogenetic DNA
2. Family (psychosocial) influence
3. Culture (sociocultural) or following dominant social norms
4. Accumulated learning and life experiences (biographic history)
5. Current situation and context (environmental)

These five meaning antecedents give each person their unique identity, including the *meaning of life* (IMDS) imprint. The individual is not always aware of what that meaning is. Nonetheless, it guides decisions and actions. As stated previously, a person operates from a *default* meaning of life when it is not willfully self-determined. In other words, the individual has not adequately explored the validity and usefulness of influencing meanings (i.e., Attributes, Beliefs, Values, Feelings, Attitudes, and Aims) or taken steps to determine their meaning of life. Another way of viewing and studying meanings is by verifying how self-determined they are. Hence, meaning-sets can be default and self-determined. Logoteleologists help clients discover their operating meaning of life (IMDS), assess its quality, and, when required, improve its content.

The quality of the IMDS influences, in turn, the type and quality of daily interactions. Let's return to Mary's case. Suppose Mary's identity meaning DNA has a reliable value system and attribution of being a responsible person and an unbending faith and confidence in her capacity to succeed. In that case, she could have a very positive Attitude (MT) and matching Feelings (MT), such as courage. Note that Mary's unbending faith in confidence is indicative of her Beliefs (MT). As this example demonstrates, her MTs agree.

Why are Meaning-construct and Sets Relevant?

Logoteleologists use meaning-constructs and sets to understand personality and assess how people perceive situations, solve problems, and approach life. While the meaning-construct is used as a theoretical model for educational, research, and practical purposes, meaning-set (i.e., a person's meaning content) analysis has application in therapy, coaching, counseling, mentoring, and consulting. In addition, meaning-set analysis is employed to diagnose and improve individual, group, organizational, national, and international meanings.

Anyone can self-assess how they approach (or could approach) situations through the MTs definitions and roles. For instance, if you were to analyze the fictitious university student, Mary, what questions could you ask yourself to dissect the situation and understand Mary's behavior? The following are six suggested questions, each for a meaning type. Take note that the first five speak to the reason of the meaning, while the sixth (Aims) relates to the intention or goal.

1. How did you *feel* when you saw the professor? (Feelings meaning type)
2. "When you saw the professor, was your impulse to approach or avoid him?" (Attitudes meaning type)
3. What rule, norm, or standard were you violating that led you to run away from the professor? (Values meaning type)
4. What opinion did you have of yourself that led you to avoid the professor? (Attributions meaning type)

5. Imagine that you had approached the professor; what explanation could you have given for submitting your paper late? (Beliefs meaning type)
6. Why did you hide? (Aims meaning type)

The answers to such sample questions are a rich source of data. Applying a meaning lens to the situation helps us to look deeper into Mary's thought process. It can also help us appreciate how recurring patterns influence behavior. For instance, if you were Mary, you could ask yourself:

- Why do I sometimes find it challenging to follow through on my commitments?
- Do I have a well-thought-out and validated code of ethics that guides my decision-making? What do I stand for? How do I define "being responsible?"
- What opinion do I have of myself that explains the need to hide from others and pretend to be someone other than me?
- What opinion do I have of others, and how do those opinions influence how I behave toward them?
- Why am I feeling so miserable?
- What do the answers to the previous questions say about the meaning and quality of my life?
- How can I come out whole?

Honest answers to insightful questions can:

- Tell us where we are (and where we want to go) in our life journey
- Assess the quality of our life
- Expose who we (truly) are
- Guide us to determine who we want to be (and not be)
- Differentiate between who we claim to be and how we behave
- Define what we want to accomplish in life (and help us discern what we do that doesn't fit those goals)
- Help us plan how to improve
- Give us control of our lives
- Assist in determining our strategy to thrive in life

To conclude, we propose that a well-facilitated Meaning-set Analysis can be a gateway to greater self-awareness, presence, mindfulness, self-regulation, and life-long success for those who are willing.

Chapter Summary and Review

Meaning

Meaning is what makes thinking and feeling possible. It allows us to define and recognize things, individuals, and concepts. It also allows us to effectively exchange information, understand and make sense of situations, and cooperate. Meanings, too, evaluate and convey the significance we attribute to concepts, things, and people.

Meaning performs two tasks: to justify (context) and determine an aim (intention/goal). Said differently, *reasons, justifications, and motives precede and produce the aim.* We can thus conclude, human conflicts, intractable problems, and many mental disturbances derive from flawed reasons and justifications. However, human thriving, success, and happiness derive from healthy and intelligent reasons and justifications. Hence, meanings may have positive or negative consequences.

There are six types of meanings in the *meaning-construct*, Attributes, Beliefs, Values, Feelings, Attitudes, and Aims. MTs are known as a meaning-set when organized as an interactive collective. The meaning-set justifies and gives intent to behavior.

Every person has an Identity Meaning-DNA Set (IMDS) that defines who they are and help predict life's potential outcomes. A known IMDS can be examined, validated, and, when required, improved. However, when the IMDS operates at an unaware level, exploring and proving its effectiveness isn't easy. Either option, aware or unaware, has consequences, but a self-determined IMDS promises more control and influence (i.e., self-determination). Conversely, an unknown IMDS risk being influenced by others' determination.

There are two types of meaning-sets: *Identity and Situational*

The identity meaning-DNA Set (IMDS):

- Reveals the operating *meaning of life*
  - The working meaning of life answers the sample question, "I am living my life as if…."
- Explains the quality of life
  - The quality of life can be better understood through rating the statement "I am happy with my life," with a response that falls somewhere on a range between "strongly agree" to "strongly disagree."
  - Improvement first requires analyzing the solution content of the IMDS.
- Is a constant and predictable meaning of life
  - The stable and consistent nature of the IMDS stands in contrast to the comparably dynamic SMS, yet, as mentioned previously, through careful observation, they can reveal the patterns of the IMDS or meaning of life."
  - The relatively static nature of the IMDS allows for patterns to be revealed through careful observation

The second type of meaning-set is the Situational Meaning-set (SMS)

- Situational Meaning-sets (SMS) are transient and based on context
  - The SMS is reactive to situations as they emerge and demand an answer
  - Responses are the outcomes of reasons, motives, or justifications
  - Observing SMS patterns can reveal the IMDS

Meaning antecedents shape the IMDS: our biogenetic, psychosocial (e.g., family), socio-cultural (e.g., culture), biographic history (e.g., life experiences), and context imprint.

Finally, there are two types of Identity Meaning DNA Sets: *default* and *self-determined*

1. A *default* IMDS has the following attributes
   a. Autopilot: Some behavior is regulated by unexplored and unverified meanings (i.e., introjects, ignorance, and blind spots).
   b. Extrinsic: some of the motives are imposed, rather than freely chosen
   c. Malleable: "default" does not mean fixed. Through self-awareness, default meanings can be replaced with healthy self-determined options
2. A healthy *self-determined* IMDS has the following attributes
   a. Free will: behavior is decided without compulsion
   b. Unbiased: strives to be impartial and acts on evidence-based truth and reality
   c. Learns: acquires meaningful knowledge to achieve and thrive
   d. Robust: meaning content is intelligent and wholesome
   e. Intrinsic: Motivation is internally derived

Introjection: an unconscious psychic process by which a person incorporates into his or her own psychic apparatus the characteristics of another person or object.

~www.thefreedictionary.com~ [28]

As stated, compared with the dynamic SMS, the IMDS is more constant and predictable. However, the content of the MTs can be modified. For instance, over time, as people mature with age and experience, the IMDS adds new information (e.g., knowledge), replacing and granting prominence to some MTs over others. This natural progression modifies and eventually influences future behavior. A person with a strong work ethic (Values MT), for example, could have been consistently encouraged to continue doing what works well. For the most part, we can expect that the daily dynamics of the SMS will be aligned with the IDMS.

Reflection and Practice

1. This chapter showed that meaning involves communicating an intention or commitment to do something based on motives, reasons,

and justifications. Recall a recent situation that is fresh in your mind. What kind of communication was involved? What reasons and aims did that communication carry?

2. Can you think of a time when a "misunderstanding" resulted from a disconnect in meaning? What was conveyed? Where was the breakdown in understanding?

3. Earlier in the chapter, we read of the mother who called her son at college regularly to check in on him. This example illustrated a classic misunderstanding or a breakdown of intention versus perception. First, from the mother's point of view, consider the meaning she aimed to convey. Then, using the six MTs, what might be an example of each contributing to making up her meaning?

4. We learned two types of meaning-sets, Situational (SMS) and Identity Meaning-DNA (IMDS). For example, consider a man standing outside of a voting location on Election Day being interviewed by a reporter whom he tells that he is a Republican. To which meaning-set does "Republican" apply?

5. Using the five meaning antecedents that make up your own Identity Meaning-DNA Set (IMDS), give an example of each.

Chapter Two

What is Meaningful and Important?

> *"A true test of character isn't how you are on your best
> days but how you act on your worst days."*
>
> *~ Anonymous ~* [29]

After reading this chapter, you will be able to...

- Understand yearning for meaning as an intrinsic human tendency
- Define and apply the Five Meaningful Life Strivings
- Recognize and apply the competencies of ACT: Allow, Cooperate, Transcend
- Identify and differentiate between Meaningful, Meaningless, Important, and Unimportant

What if we could build over time the ability and confidence to select the right choice when making people-related decisions? Is there a method to simplify decision-making to help us reach the correct conclusions? Meaningful purpose psychology (MP) helps people make wise and mutually beneficial decisions. Let us see how.

Humans Yearn the Meaningful

> *"Personal strivings thus represent the characteristic goals that
> a person strives for during his or her everyday life."*
>
> *~Richard M. Ryan, et al.~* [30]

People strive for what is meaningful in life. The *meaningful* is positive, mutually beneficial, transcendental, altruistic, virtuous, and replenishing. You can sense when you are or have been in a meaningful state or experience because it meets one or more of the following five conditions:

1. **Love:** You and those around you care for and respect one another
2. **Peace and peace of mind:** You feel safe, protected, and in harmony with your environment and those you share it with. You feel assured that those around you "have your back."
3. **Happiness:** You are mindful of (and grateful for) the good in your life and are content and satisfied
4. **Engagement:** You are committed to those around you, the pursuits you take up, and the people with whom you choose to spend your time
5. **Prosperity:** You connect to the value in your life and use that connection to build on that value for you and others intellectually, spiritually, financially, emotionally, and experientially

These are five meaningful states that humans yearn for and strive to experience in life. Named *The Five Meaningful Life Strivings* or *The Meaningful Path* due to their aspirational and progressive natures, fulfilling those five states gives life an uplifting meaning.

The Five Meaningful Life Strivings can

- Provide joy, safety, and support
- Uplift and bring out the best in the self and others
- Inspire peace and balance internally and in surroundings
- Increase the likelihood of a healthy and prosperous future

For further helpful reading, we encourage you to review the PERMA[31] and IKAGAI[32] Models.

"Transformational leadership occurs when one or more people engage with others in such a way that leaders and followers elevate each other to higher levels of motivation and morality."

- James MacGregor Burns - [33]

ACT: The Three Pillars of Meaningful Purpose

Fulfilling the *Five Meaningful Life Strivings* puts a person well on their way down the path to a meaningful purpose, but real success cannot be achieved through an inward focus alone. It also depends on the ability to ACT within our surroundings and the environment we share. In other words, to be other-oriented. [34] We can do so through the following practices:

- **A**llow: Supporting others' inherent right to achieve their individuality and potential
- **C**ooperate: Where members of a community or team leverage their strengths and talents to achieve a common goal harmoniously and for a noble cause
- **T**ranscend: Individual or group members dedicate themselves to practice selfless actions for a noble cause to benefit others

Consider a person who is pursuing wealth at any cost. Firmly committed to the prospect of a life secure and fulfilled, they are well aware of the benefits and fortunes they enjoy. Yet, this person ruthlessly grows their coffers and all the wealth that entails at others' expense. How likely is it that this person can find a truly meaningful and prosperous experience when they cause such imbalance and disharmony in their surroundings? The path to a meaningful purpose needs to account for others and our surroundings. Without *ACT*, the pursuit of the five strivings is met with environmental discord that can easily impede achieving real meaningfulness.

Following the Five Meaningful Life Strivings and practicing ACT leads to life fulfillment. They also have specific benefits when applied to business, organizational, or other group settings. Firmly committed to the proper pursuit of both the strivings and *ACT* can be the difference between engaged or just showing up, leading the way or lagging, determined or despondent, even good or great. The adage that by helping others, we help ourselves speaks to the benefit of *ACT* in achieving the *Five Meaningful Life Strivings*. Ultimately, developing and mastering the competencies of Allowing, Cooperating, and Transcending makes possible the fulfillment of the Five Meaningful Life Strivings.

Apply MP!

Consider the example of a group in a meeting where there is concern about the boss' particularly volatile temper. The task of the group becomes secondary to the objective of managing the behavior of the boss. In this way, the group is unable to achieve the meaningful outcomes they pursue fully. The group lacks team spirit and cohesion (part of the "love" striving). Therefore conflict is created (lack of peace and peace of mind for group participants), preventing complete and genuine engagement. If the group were to prioritize the five strivings of Love, Peace, Happiness, Engagement, and Prosperity, they would have achieved their goals through a gratifying experience without the unnecessary and ultimately disruptive drama.

Contrasting the Meaningful with the Meaningless

"We hold these Truths to be self-evident, that all Men are created equal, that they are endowed by their Creator with certain unalienable Rights, that among these are Life, Liberty, and the Pursuit of Happiness"

-Thomas Jefferson, U.S. Declaration of Independence-

In MP theory and method, the *meaningful* builds, enhances, and points to what is significant and beneficial. In meaningful environments, life doesn't consist of winners and losers. People are concerned for one another, and no one goes lacking. Being part of a meaningful culture entails being genuine, responsible, dependable, and accountable. People grow because members are committed to remaining self-aware, following meaningful standards, and improving as individuals, teams, and organizations. Decision-makers select choices that prove to be meaningful over time. In other words, the choice will have a meaningful benefit today, tomorrow, and beyond. Over time, what is *meaningful* is both sustainable and beneficial to all stakeholders. All concerned accept that virtuous people development produces positive relationships, healthy families, communities, and business excellence. In meaningful environments, people thrive and become better, happy, and more productive human beings.

In contrast, the *meaningless* is the antithesis of the *meaningful*. Dictionary. com defines meaningless as "without meaning, significance, purpose, or value, purposeless, insignificant." [35] In MP, the *meaningless* is inconsiderate, demeaning, petty, empty, and insignificant. Not surprisingly, *meaningless* conditions can lead to a winner/loser life dichotomy. The environment is tainted with distrust and suspicion, and the functional approach is one of a competitive "survival."

History has shown that cultures rooted in or predicated upon *meaninglessness* force members into submission, strict obedience to rigid rules and policies, and involuntary compliance, generating passive and even active resistance.

In such meaningless environments, individuals are likely to do the bare minimum demanded of them, barely carrying out their prescribed duties, and are unwilling to serve any common good. Decisions are shortsighted and myopic, and instant gratification sacrifices the potential benefits of a mid to long-term viewpoint. Meaningless settings are contentious, stressful, exhausting, and depleting.

Why is the contrast between Meaningful and Meaningless relevant?

The *meaningful* serves the common good, while the *meaningless* is corrosive and should be avoided whenever possible. That is why MP practitioners are inclined to study and research findings from various fields, particularly psychology, to generate and propose practical and scientifically well-founded solutions toward human success and prosperity.

Understanding the difference between what is *meaningful* and what is *meaningless* can:

1. Enhance autonomy and self-determination
2. Build a confident set of values to live by
3. Disentangle knowing what does and does not require our attention and choice
4. Simplify decision making
5. Promote prosocial benefits and consequences

What is Important and Unimportant?

Important equates to having priorities and giving significance. The *important* activates our attention, demands selectivity, and ranking among options. [36] Knowing what is *important* allows us to prioritize and grant prominence. On the other hand, the *unimportant* is categorized as low-ranking, insignificant, inconsequential, and irrelevant—the *unimportant* calls for low (or no) attention.

In meaningful purpose psychology (MP) theory, "important" does not equate to "meaningful." Nor does "unimportant" equal "meaningless." Thus, in the MP method, a person can give *importance* to the *meaningless,* though it could go without saying that they should not.

	Meaningful	Meaningless
Important	Willed to Improve, Uplift and Edify	Driven to Degrade, Demean and Demoralize
Unimportant	Neglect to Improve, Uplift and Edify	Reject Degrading, Demeaning and Demoralizing

Figure 3 Meaningful / Important Quadrant

Figure 3 presents four behavioral options individuals and institutions can follow and apply.

1. *The important and meaningful displays behavior that is intended to edify and improve.* For instance, we can choose to recognize a peer for a job well done or a child for making good choices.
2. *The unimportant and meaningless indicate behavior that avoids demeaning others.* Thus, we decide not to infer that our theory and method are better than others' approaches.
3. *The important and meaningless bears out behavior designed to demean and degrade people,* as in the case of a bully in a schoolyard who verbally and physically abuses others.

Key Learning Points

The Five Meaningful Life Strivings

1. Love
2. Peace and peace of mind
3. Happiness
4. Engagement
5. Prosperity

The meaningful is positive, mutually beneficial, transcendental, altruistic, virtuous, and replenishing.

The meaningless is something or someone we could consider useless, trivial, worthless, insignificant, as well as having low value.

Four behavioral options individuals and institutions can follow and apply.

1. The important and meaningful displays behavior intended to edify and improve.
2. The unimportant and meaningless indicate behavior that avoids demeaning others.
3. The important and meaningless bears out action intended to demean and degrade people.
4. The unimportant and meaningful reveals behavior that neglects to build and edify others.

In MP theory, importance does not mean meaningful. Nor does "unimportant" parallel "meaningless."

4. *The unimportant and meaningful reveals behavior that neglects to build and edify others,* as is when a person chooses to disregard acknowledging another for their excellent performance. Or said differently, the person does not give importance to doing what is good for themselves and others.

Based on these explanations, options one and two are more acceptable and worthwhile. Options three and four should be avoided at all costs.

Why is the contrast between Important and Unimportant relevant?

Again, in MP theory, *importance* does not mean *meaningful*. While it is possible (and desirable) to give importance or prominence to what is meaningful, as shown, it is also possible to provide vast importance to the meaningless by demeaning others, as in the case of bullying or by objectifying fellow human beings through conflict.

Sadly, every day and in all corners of this world, people miss opportunities to do good for others; and fail to encourage and build up when called to do so.

These definitions and contrasts are relevant here in that they show the value in choosing what is *important* over what is *unimportant, meaningful* over what is *meaningless,* and the benefits. They simplify decision-making by telling us which two options will serve us best and which two we should avoid. The science behind this conclusion is robust.

Chapter Summary and Review

Humans yearn for meaning and pursue meaningful conditions. This pursuit is referred to as *The Five Meaningful Life Strivings* or *The Meaningful Path.*

1. Love
2. Peace and peace of mind
3. Happiness
4. Engagement
5. Prosperity

The Five Strivings are fulfilled through the three pillars of Meaningful Purpose: Allow, Cooperate, and Transcend (ACT). Together the Five Strivings and ACT can make life meaningful and support a worthwhile meaning of life.

That which is meaningful builds, enhances, and highlights what is significant and beneficial. Meaningfulness is constructive, uplifting, positive, and practical.

That which is meaningless is useless, trivial, worthless, insignificant, and has low value or regard. Meaninglessness is negative, empty, and limiting. Devoid of inspiration, the meaningless is a destructive and unsatisfying opposing force.

In MP, the term "important" does not equate to "meaningful," and "unimportant" is not the same as "meaningless." Every person, when interacting with others, is faced with four options, each with consequence; and that is to grant

1. Importance to the meaningful
2. Importance to the meaningless
3. Low or no importance to the meaningful
4. Low or no importance to the meaningless

Giving prominence to the meaningful and giving little or none to the meaningless can lead to meaningful relationships, environments, organizations, and cultures.

Reflection and Practice

1. Using an example of something meaningful from your life, a job or field of study, a relationship, or a hobby, describe the relationship it has to one or more of the Five Meaningful Life Strivings.
2. Pick one section from the meaningful/important quadrant in Chapter Two and describe an example that illustrates it.
3. How can something one considers important also be meaningless? Why might someone place importance on something meaningless?

4. As an exercise, list ten things that you did today. They could be made up of places gone, things said, activities engaged in, etc. Then indicate whether they were meaningful or meaningless. Did you find that some of what you have done you would characterize as insignificant? What consequence might this meaningless have, say, on your mood, productivity, or otherwise?

Chapter Three

The Identity Formula

Who am I?

"Be yourself; everyone else is already taken."

~Oscar Wilde~ [37]

How would you describe yourself? What does it mean to be you? How are you getting along in life? How satisfactory and fulfilling has your life been?

If the spirit of these questions, after reading this chapter, you will be able to...

- Define identity
- Understand and differentiate between the three types of identities
- Explain how identities are formed and why they matter
- Distinguish between Person, Social, and Role identity meaning-sets
- Comprehend and apply the Logoteleology Identity Model

Identity Defined

Identity is what makes us uniquely recognizable to ourselves and others. In other words, identity is how we self-describe and how others describe our personality and physical features. For example, when we complete the sentence "I am _____," we express our self-concept or how we view ourselves. As will be explained later in greater detail, *identities reveal our meaning of life.*

Three Types of Identity

According to sociologists Peter J. Burke and Jan E. Stets' *Identity Theory* [38], there are three types of identities: person, group, and role. We all have these three types of identities.

Person Identity

> *"Person identities are based on a view of the person as a unique identity, distinct from other individuals."*
>
> ~ *Peter J. Burke and Jan E. Stets* ~ [39]

Person identity is formed in early life by our DNA, family, culture, life experiences, expectations we place on ourselves, and continuous learning and improvement. Person identity is not static but is dynamic, developmental, and adaptable to circumstances. Everyone has their sole "meaning imprint," or a collection of interdependent MTs (recall from Chapter One the meaning-construct) that makes them an individual. No one has your exact biological DNA or unique history, nor do they have the same potential. You are the only version of you that has been or will ever be. That makes you extraordinary, unique, and special. Your distinct and unique person identity with all its potentiality cannot be duplicated. Fortunately, you are not expected by life to be an impersonator, or worse yet, an impostor because you are unique. What makes each life exceptional is that no person can take another's place or fulfill the duty that life asks them to perform. Think about it: there is, and will only be, one model of each human being—past, present, and future. There is only one of you. What you are called to do in life, no one can do in your stead.

A person's identity has physical (body) and psychological (mind) dimensions. In this whole lies the individual's self-concept—how the person presents and explains themself.

Finally, person identities are important because they hold the individual's *meaning of life* and show what gives life meaning (i.e., *meaning in life*), a subject we will cover later in the book.

Social (Group) Identity

As social beings, people associate and want to be part of a group. For the most part, we all share the need to relate. Social identity has group members describe themselves in terms of "us," or the in-group, in contrast to "them," or the out-group. Social identity, by default, leads to in-group/out-group behavior. Being a group member can provide members a sense of solidarity through shared interests, experiences, values, beliefs, and feelings. By contrast, those outside the group *could* have conflicting aims and values and, as a result, be considered opponents. Hence, being or not being a part of a social group can have positive and negative effects.

Not all our social memberships are voluntary. People can also end up in the social identity category by default or obligation. Here we break social identity into three parts, the *default social identity*, the *obligatory social identity*, and the *voluntary social identity*. The statements characterize the three subcategories of social identity, "I was born into...", "I have to...", and "I choose to..." respectively.

Default Social Identity

"I WAS BORN INTO..."

We are all born into default groups. Default social identities include race, gender, place of origin, nationality, family or clan, and religious membership. In vernacular language, we are "stuck" with the default identities we inherit at the time of birth—at least for a time and not without facing potential difficulty changing those identities.

Default memberships can be a source of pride. For instance, consider the euphoric feeling when fellow compatriots win a medal in the Olympic games. Yet, default memberships also have a dark side: they can trigger divisiveness through discriminatory categorization. In extreme cases, they lead to political conflict and war.

Other possible examples that could indicate *default social identity* is when we say: "I was raised as...", "Where I'm from, we...", and "I'm from the...."

Key Learning Points

Identity is how we self-describe and how others describe our character or personality and physical features. There are three types of identities: person, group, and role. (Peter J. Burke and Jan E. Stets)

Five meaning antecedents form identities:

1. Our biogenetic DNA
2. Family (psychosocial) influence
3. Culture (sociocultural) or following dominant social norms
4. Accumulated learning and life experiences (biographic history)
5. Current situation and context

Identity has three components: Meaning, Motivation, and Purpose.

$I = Me + Mo + P$

- Meaning (gr. logos) answers, "why?"
- Motivation (gr. thelos) answers, "How willing am I?"
- Purpose (gr. telos) answers, "What and how I will do it."

Identities

1. Give meaning to life
2. Allow us to be autonomous, self-regulate and do what matters
3. Set us apart from others
4. Remind us of our common humanity
5. Expresses and fulfills what is meaningful to us
6. Fulfill our affiliation needs
7. Help us succeed

Obligatory Social Identity

"I HAVE TO"

As the title suggests, *obligatory social identities* are generally imposed by external pressure. For instance, an employee can be "volunteered" to be in a committee regardless of interest and desire, with a negative consequence imposed if participation is refused. Because this type of membership is involuntary, the perceived imposed expectation can be resented and resisted. And while resistance might fluctuate within a like/don't like continuum (i.e., the Attitudes meaning type), it is resistance nonetheless. And that is what makes the obligatory membership potentially unpleasant and counterproductive, mainly if it is overused.

Voluntary Social Identity

"I CHOOSE TO..."

Voluntary participation involves affiliations of our choosing and our own free will. For instance, one can choose to join a company as an employee, belong to a religious denomination, be a club member, decide one's career path, and associate with valued friends. Equally powerful is choosing not to engage in these, which is also part of the *voluntary social identity*.

Meaningful purpose psychology (MP) claims that voluntary identities, where members willingly join and freely express themselves to achieve common goals, are more sustainable, engaging, and productive than forced through *obligatory social identities*.

Temporary and Lasting Groups

Not all groups that people belong to are the same. There are differences in how some groups function, what brings members into the group in the first place, and how they operate within them. A group could fall into two categories: *informal and temporary* or *formal and lasting*. The first category, *informal and temporary*, comes about through casual and short-lived interactions.

One example of this category is a group of strangers on board an airplane. The passengers on the flight are grouped through some commonalities. The passengers are in the same airport and going to a common destination (at least in the near term). While there is no doubt that the situation they find themselves in has made them a group, membership is causal. It will last about as long as the flight, at which point the group members will part ways and potentially never see one another again. The members do not necessarily contribute to the group or fulfill specific group roles, which would be much more common in the *formal and lasting* group.

The second category, *formal and lasting* groups, applies when people come together to fulfill a common task that requires investment in resources, such as time and diligent effort. To accomplish the shared goals, members must decide who will do what, how, and when. Role clarification is done through the organization and assignment of responsibilities. Role clarification produces a *role identity* that group members will use to identify themselves and others in the group and to each other as individuals within the group.

Role Identity

Role identities are a subset of social identities (e.g., groups). A role identity has a title, such as president, secretary, mother, wife, husband, firstborn, grandparent, sibling, etc. A role identity has duties to fulfill, requires abilities and personal traits to do well, and must interact with other group members (e.g., interdependence) to achieve the assumed common task. The role's expectations determine what it means (and requires) to fill that position, for example, a spouse, a son or daughter, the committee chair, a friend, a third baseman, a team lead, or a bus driver.

Role identity is defined as a position within a group requiring skills and attributes to perform assigned duties alongside and coordinating with other group members to fulfill a goal or mission to provide a service or generate a benefit.

Because role identities are a subset of social identities, they are subject to fall into one of three option states: default, obligatory, and voluntary. The explanations and context of those subsets of social identity apply to role identities as well.

Role identities have a dark and meaningless side. Roles such as mugger, inquisitor, and terrorist are examples of occupants with a hostile and meaningless agenda.

Person, Social, and Role Identity Meaning-sets

Person, social, and role identities (PSRI) have meaning-sets. Later in the chapter, we will discuss this concept further in the Logoteleology Identity Model or LIM context. The effectiveness and contribution of a PSRI meaning-set depend on its content and quality. The outputs (i.e., aims) of the PSRI meaning-set can be meaningful as well as meaningless.

Family members, social and religious circles, national culture, formal education, and life experiences form, improve, and develop healthy PSRI meaning-sets. However, when these identity-shaping sources fail to produce healthy PSRI's, by default, their meaning-sets will bring about negative consequences. People can prevent these meaningless outcomes by building and following meaningful goals, particularly aligned with The Five Meaningful Life Strivings (i.e., The Meaningful Path).

Remedial support is a specialized service for each identity type that may be needed, particularly when preventive methods are not followed. For example, coaching, therapy, or some other approach to help address the flawed meaning. As a rule, coaches, therapists, and counselors assist with person identity (i.e., individual) problems, while consultants typically help with dysfunctional social and role identities (e.g., teams and organizations).

> **Remedial Support:** *a specialized support service for each identity type required when preventative methods are not followed.*

	Defined	Default	Obligatory	Voluntary
Person	A person's unique identity. Answers, "Who am I?"	Born into. Agrees, "This is who (I was told) I am."	Imposed and expected. External entities state, "This is who you are."	Self-determined. Affirms, "This is who I am."
Social	Group membership. Answers, "Where do I belong?"	Born into. Accepts, "This is where I belong."	Imposed and expected. External entities asserts, "This is where you will belong."	Self-determined. Decides, "This is where I choose to belong."
Role	The function assumed within a group. Answers, "How will I contribute?"	Born into and delegated. Acknowledges, "This is how I contribute."	Imposed and expected. External entities declares, "These are your duties within the group."	Self-determined. Pronounces, "This is what I choose to do."

Table 4 Types of Identities [40]

Apply MP!

Your person identity affects how you experience and interact in a social context and your roles. For example, coaching, therapy, or some other approach to help address the flawed meaning. You bring this person identity to whatever situations you engage in, as these are where your social and role identities play out. Having a clear sense of who you are, and participating in a way that aligns well with that identity, boosts the odds that you'll achieve your most beneficial outcomes. These positive results are realized when your person identity is clear to you and optimized in a way that maximizes connections to the Five Meaningful Life Strivings. With your clear sense of this person identity, you can then seek opportunities to connect to it in your relationships and social involvements. Doing this will result in feeling more connected and fulfilled through these experiences.

How Are Identities Formed?

In the first chapter, we learned that every human being has a unique *meaning imprint* or *meaning DNA*. Worth repeating, this meaning imprint is a construct or collection of interdependent MTs (Attributes, Beliefs, Values, Attitudes, Feelings, and Aims) called a *meaning-set*. This meaning imprint or DNA is the content and essence of personality or identity. The previously discussed meaning antecedents shape the identity through:

1. Our biogenetic DNA

2. Family (psychosocial) influence
3. Culture (sociocultural) or following dominant social norms
4. Accumulated learning and life experiences (biographic history)
5. Current situation and context

From birth, humans have their biogenetic imprint or DNA (person identity). We learn and grow within the context of our family and cultural environments (social identity). For the most part, we adapt and respond to our expectations as members of our communities (role identity). Ideally, over time, as children move toward adulthood, they gain the necessary knowledge and abilities to contribute to the social good. However, limiting conditions can deprive people of fulfilling their potential.

MP can be used to build environments where humans can thrive and reach their full potential. As previously covered, such ideal conditions are best achieved through the Five Meaningful Life Strivings: Love, Peace, Happiness, Engagement, and Prosperity and ACT (Allow, Cooperate, and Transcend). A strong understanding of and attention to these crucial focuses can make life worth living and give life meaning.

We also encourage individuals to pay attention to the meaning they have given to themselves, others, and situations or, in short, the meaning they have given to life. Attention requires being aware, analyzing, and validating the quality of their Meaning DNA, as well as their meaning mindset and worldview. Certified Logoteleologists help individuals, teams, and organizations uncover, analyze, validate, and improve identity meaning-sets.

The Logoteleology Identity Model

Now that we know the genesis of identities, what makes an identity according to MP (logoteleology)?

Identity has three components: Meaning, Motivation, and Purpose. Hence, the formula:

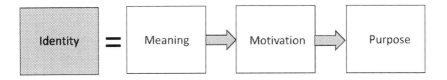

Figure 4 Logoteleology Identity Model

Or

$$I = Me + Mo + P$$

Grammatically, *identities* are expressed as nouns (i.e., man, accountant) or pronouns (i.e., She).

Meanings provide the "why" behind the action. Remember from our first chapter that meaning-sets, through a mental process, fulfill two tasks: (1) generate reasons and justifications in order to (2) determine an aim or intention. Therefore, Meanings set the behavioral agenda.

> *"... to have an intention is not only to have a reason to act but also to have a body oriented toward a goal."*
>
> *~ Dorothée Legrand ~* [41]

Motivation determines the meaning's assigned level and type of commitment. Describing how willing I am to perform a task, such as "slightly interested" or "very committed," are examples. We generally can deduce a person's motivation or "motive to action" by the amount of energy invested in their action (or inaction) and their perseverance or resolve.

Purpose is conveyed through action verbs such as print, consult, teach, and build. Purpose determines *what* and *how* tasks will be achieved. Purpose is the domain of applied competence. Important to note here is the difference between *meaning* and *purpose*. Put simply, meaning determines the reason and intention for an action, and purpose carries it out. "I read to understand because I value learning" is an illustration of a purpose with a meaning justification. The word "read" being the action (purpose) and the terms "understand" and "learning" speak to the intention and the reason, respectively. This example also provides the meaning type (values) for the reasoning. We can infer from the previous statement that the motivation is such that the reader is inclined toward the action (will, more on this in Chapter Four). Some simple additions to the statement can speak to the type and level of motivation; "I read often because I highly value learning." The words "often" and "highly" indicate a high level of motivation toward the action. *Motivation propels purpose to fulfill meanings.*

> *"The* purpose *is the aim of the meaning as a concept, the point under meaningful expression, the very essence of what is being conveyed. Framed in causal terms, purpose takes its meaning from formal causation, as in the final-cause definition where it represents the 'that' in the 'that for the sake of which' phrasing."*

> *"Purpose may be thought of as the reason a certain intention is enacted.* Intention *refers to the remaining 'for the sake of which' phrasing of the final-cause definition. Intentions enliven or create the 'that's' (purposes) in words, images, assessments, and most important of all, actions. To mean is to intend."*

> *~ Joseph F. Rychlack ~* [42]

Let's use Curtis as an example. Curtis loves his job, and when asked what he does for a living, he replies:

> "I am a weather forecaster who deeply enjoys reporting weather conditions to help people plan their daily lives."

Using the identity formula, we can break this statement down to understand the Logoteleology Identity Model (LIM) as it relates to Curtis' own identity:

- Identity: The label or name of the identity = *"weather forecaster."*
- Purpose: What you do = *"reporting weather conditions."*
- Motivation: Enthusiasm toward carrying out the action = *"deeply enjoys."*
- Meaning: Reason and intention = *"to help people plan their daily lives."*

Consultants, therapists, and coaches use the logoteleology identity formula to help organizations, teams, and individuals to assess and improve the quality of their meanings, motivations, and abilities. MP practitioners (Logoteleologists) determine the

- quality and strength of each element of the identity model. For instance,
  - o Is the meaning-set well-informed?
  - o Is there a commitment to move forward?
  - o Are there the right competencies to act and succeed?
- degree of agreement and congruence among the three elements. For instance, a person can have the best of meaning intentions yet fails because they lack the skills to accomplish the aim.

The Logoteleology Identity Model in Action

Because identities are social and fulfill expectations through roles, the Logoteleology Identity Model (LIM) can also study interpersonal transactions, impact, and consequences. Figure 5 is the expanded version of the Identity Model.

When transacting with others, we pay attention to five components: Meaning, Motivation, Purpose, Contact, Consequence, and Feedback. These are the elements of the Logoteleology Identity Model in Action (LIMA) and are explained through the formula:

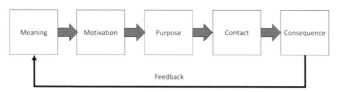

Figure 5 The Logoteleology Identity Model in Action (LIMA)

Or

LIMA

I = Me + Mo + P + Co -> C

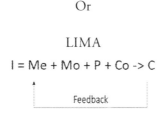

The components of meaning, motivation, and purpose make the identity. We described these three in the previous section as critical elements of the LIM. Meaning, Motivation, and Purpose fall under the control of the identity. The two components, *contact* and *consequence,* are external to the identity. Therefore, the identity can be and is influenced by contact and consequence.

Contact

Contact relates to the target of our attention and the overall context and setting. Purposeful actions impact the environment and its stakeholders. Purposeful activities, too, will vary depending on conditions and who the stakeholders are. For instance, a person who is upset at his mother in a private setting could react differently than how he would respond to being upset with his direct manager in a Board meeting. Context influences meanings and purposeful action.

Key Learning Points

The Logoteleology Identity Model in Action (LIMA) has six components

1. Meaning
2. Motivation
3. Purpose
4. Contact
5. Consequence
6. Feedback

Contact refers to the operating context, setting, and stakeholders. Understanding the target of our aims is essential because people can respond differently based on the environment, context, and stakeholders.

Consequence explains how the intended meaning and expressed purpose impacted the setting, context, and stakeholders, including self and others.

There are four possible consequences. Logoteleologists help clients improve decision-making through the Intended-Outcome Model. (See Figure 6 The Intended Outcome Model)

Feedback answers the question: "Did my intended meaning met its aim?" Feedback is an operating element of a self-regulating system, including an identity.

Consequence

Consequence reveals how the contact responded. The response will fall somewhere on the scales of *intention* and *outcome*; this is known as the Intended-Outcome Model (*Figure 6*). For instance, an expected consequence could include intimidating another person with a weapon; the unexpected consequence could be being arrested for threatening another's life. Logoteleologists use the Intended-Outcome Model to diagnose and improve option selection.

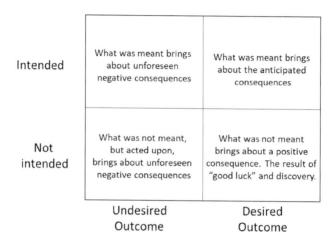

	Undesired Outcome	Desired Outcome
Intended	What was meant brings about unforeseen negative consequences	What was meant brings about the anticipated consequences
Not intended	What was not meant, but acted upon, brings about unforeseen negative consequences	What was not meant brings about a positive consequence. The result of "good luck" and discovery.

Figure 6 The Intended-Outcome Model

As shown in Figure 6, clients learn that there are four types of consequences, sometimes expected and, at times, unexpected. Logoteleologists, or meaningful purpose psychology practitioners, help clients increase the odds of fulfilling their meaningful intentions or aims through purposeful actions.

Feedback

Finally, regarding Figure 5, and in tune with self-regulation psychology, *feedback* helps individuals determine if their meanings were fulfilled. Therapists, counselors, coaches, and consultants use this model to assess the interpersonal, group, and organizational transactions. It helps answer the question, "Did I fulfill (consequence) what I intended (meaning)?

The practitioner can use any of the six components of the Logoteleology Identity Model in Action (LIMA) as a starting point. For instance, the practitioner can work with the client to determine if the consequence matches the aimed meaning.

Diagnosing through the LIMA

The Logoteleology Identity Model (LIM) and the Logoteleology Identity Model in Action (LIMA) are used as diagnostic, validating, improvement, and corrective tools within disciplines such as coaching, therapy, counseling, and consulting. Explaining the application of the method as it applies to each field is beyond this book's scope. However, through the following illustration (Figure 7), we can demonstrate how a certified Logoteleologist listens, discerns, and helps clients employing the Logoteleology Identity Model in Action.

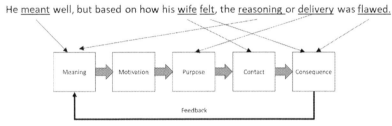

Figure 7 Diagnosing through the Identity Model in Action

As the illustration demonstrates, the Logoteleologist dissects the statements to discern how the client means and acts and what impact behavior has on others. Notice, through the arrows, how keywords are matched to each element. Understanding the overall context of the situation, the Logoteleologist can use any of these keywords to help the client be more aware, and eventually, more effective, precise, and meaningful in their approach. Hence, the LIMA helps with self-regulation as a psychological control system that instinctively and iteratively maintains a meaning-determined heading.

Why do Identities Matter?

Identities matter for the following eight reasons:

1. Identities provide meaning to life (i.e., your worldview).
2. You either shape or control your identity, or someone (or something) else will.
3. Identities are self-regulating and self-fulfilling. That means we are logoteleological or goal-oriented by meanings. We are psychologically designed to fulfill the meanings we hold about ourselves, others, and situations. Since the mind can operate as a GPS, we can use our self-regulating system to our advantage.
4. Identities can help us detect and follow what matters and avoid meaningless distractions.
5. Each identity contains a unique "meaning in life." This inimitable "meaning in life" inherently channels our creativity, strengths, and talents to do good for ourselves and others.
6. Your identities (person, social, and role) set you apart from others.
7. Identities remind us of our shared humanity.
8. Identities can fulfill our (affiliation) need to be a part of something.
9. Healthy identities achieve productive ends.

Chapter Summary and Review

Identity is our self-concept or how we view ourselves. Based on Burke and Stets' Identity Theory, the three types of identities are person, social, and role. A *person identity* expresses a person's uniqueness and distinction from other individuals. Also, a person identity reveals an individual's meaning of life. A *social identity* describes one's membership in a group. Groups, in turn, can have *role identities.*

Role identity is a position within a group with a distinct title requiring skills and attributes to succeed by performing assigned duties and coordinating with other group members to fulfill a goal or a mission to provide a service and generate a benefit.

Social and role identities are subject to three possible states: default, obligatory, and voluntary.

In line with the Logoteleology Identity Model (LIM), person, social, and role identities (PSRI) have meaning-sets. The content and quality of the PSRI meaning-set determine the ultimate impact and legacy to be either meaningful or meaningless. The Meaningful Path or the Five Meaningful Life Strivings can lead to a prosperous life. However, remedial support is required when preventive methods are not followed.

The Logoteleology Identity Model has three components: Meaning, Motivation, and Purpose.

- Meanings fulfill two tasks: to provide reason and intention and set the behavioral agenda.
- Motivation is energy-in-motion. Meaning determines the type and intensity of motivation.
- Purpose is the domain of competencies, where the action happens. Purposeful actions impact others or the environment. The objective of the purpose is to fulfill meanings.

The Logoteleology Identity Model in Action adds three components, contact, consequence, and feedback. Contact relates to the target of our attention and the overall context and setting. Consequence reveals how the contact responded and uses the Intended-Outcome Model. Finally, feedback is tasked to inform the meaning-set if the consequence met the meaning aim.

Certified Logoteleologists use the Logoteleology Identity Model (LIM) and the Logoteleology Identity Model in Action (LIMA) to prevent, develop, and remedy.

Reflection and Practice

- What are some of your own identities?
    - o Person:
    - o Social (group):
    - o Role:
- Pick a role you fill in your life; it can be a professional one, like Curtis the weatherman, or anything else (i.e., mother, son, leader, friend, etc.) and fill out the equation.

- o   Identity: The label or name of the identity
- o   Purpose: What do you do in this role?
- o   Motivation: How motivated are you in this role?
- o   Meaning: Why do you do it?
- Now pick two people you know and separately ask them to answer these inventory questions about a role they fill in their lives. Finally, complete the equation in the same way you did for your role.
- How was the experience breaking down the pieces of the formula?
- Did you think differently (more in-depth) about the role by breaking down the elements in this way?
- Do you, or someone you know, fill a role in life where the first two parts of the equation (Identity and Purpose) are more comfortable to answer, but it's difficult to explain the second two parts (Motivation and Meaning)?
- What might the implications of this kind of situation be on effectiveness or productivity in the role?
- How can the Intended-Outcome Model help diagnose and improve decision-making?

Chapter Four

Motivation

The Will to Meaning

> *"Striving to find meaning in one's life is the*
> *primary motivational force in man."*
>
> ~ *Viktor Frankl* ~ [43]

What is your passion? What energizes you to act? Why are you motivated to do certain things and avoid doing others? How would others describe your energy, commitment, and initiative? How do you influence others to perform? How can you increase your team's engagement and productivity?

These motivation-related questions are asked daily countless times all over the world. They are continually asked because our ability and disposition to remain motivated are vital to improving and succeeding. Organizational leaders, too, have a stake in creating conditions for an engaged workforce. Yet, the lack or wrong type of motivation is a persistent problem for many.

Yes, for many people, motivation is one of life's unresolved mysteries. New Year's resolutions, promises to exercise more, lose weight, and quit smoking are just some [lack of or misdirected] motivation-related challenges that lead so often to failure. However, once motivation is understood correctly and channeled, it can be harnessed into a powerful tool for success.

As human beings, we are always showing energy and direction and striving for meaning.[44] The quality of our motivation is determined by the strength, vigor, and health of our meanings and abilities. In short, meanings spur motivation to fuel purposeful behavior. Recall from the previous chapter the example we used to illustrate the Logoteleology Identity Model (LIM) "I read often because I highly value learning." The LIM elements, meaning, motivation, and purpose, are characterized in the words "read" (purpose), "often...highly" (motivation), and "learning" (meaning). The terms "often" and "highly" indicate the action's kind and level of energy. These words within this context show us that the person acting is doing so enthusiastically and with vigor. Suppose the statement was modified to use alternate words in the place of these motivation-related terms, for example, "I rarely read because I value learning little." In that case, you can see how the energy level and type are modified. We can infer from this language that the reader is not enthusiastic, or even interested, for that matter, in the activity. In the chapter ahead, we'll dive more into where this energy comes from and its impact on purpose.

After reading this chapter, you'll be able to...

- Define motivation through a logoteleological lens
- Understand the role motivation has in the Logoteleology Identity Model (LIM)
- Describe what triggers motivation
- Comprehend and apply meaningful purpose psychology (MP) to improve motivation

Motivation Defined

Motivation can be understood in two ways: a construct (or concept) and a process (or activity). As a construct, it has two elements, energy and direction. In this sense, motivation can be thought of as directed energy. As a process, motivation provides energy and direction to propel purpose (as per the Logoteleology Identity Model).

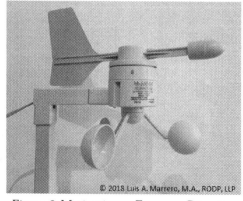

© 2018 Luis A. Marrero, M.A., RODP, LLP

Figure 8 Motivation = Energy + Direction

In this way, motivation is an activity that brings energy and direction to bear for action (purpose). The following formula explains motivation as a process:

> *Motivation = Energy + Direction*
>
> *(Mo = E + D)*

Figure 9 Logoteleology Motivation Formula

Regarding motivation as a construct, Reeve offers, "The study of motivation concerns those processes that give behavior its energy and direction." Notice Reeve's use of the terms "energy" and "direction" here. Elsewhere he states, "Motives are internal experiences—needs, cognitions, and emotions—that energize the individual's approach and avoidance tendencies. External

Figure 10 Energy / Motivational Intensity

events are environmental incentives that attract and repel the individual to engage or not engage in a particular course of action." [45] As is illustrated in this description, motivation provides energy and direction based on a *like/ don't like continuum.* [46] Approach versus avoidance, engage or don't engage are scale measurements of motivation. The direction of the motivation in the meaning-set is influenced, or determined, by the Attitudes meaning type.

> *"More than two decades of research have confirmed the idea that attitudes exert a directive influence on behavior."*
>
> *~ Icek Ajzen ~* [47]

Motivation expresses the relative importance of options. An alternative with high priority generates a higher level of motivation, while an option with low emphasis generates lower motivation levels. The degree of significance, or energy invested, is determined by the meaning-set, particularly related to the Beliefs, Feelings (e.g., the expectation of a reward), and Values (e.g., doing good for another) MTs.

Energy

Energy is defined as *available power*. We need this power to carry out the purposeful mental and physical activities assigned by meanings. We need to "burn calories," turning potential energy into kinetic energy and providing us fuel to get things done.

Energy can vary in intensity; it can range from non-existent to very high. Each of us is familiar with how energy feels and how levels of energy wax and wane throughout a day, a workweek, a conversation, etc. If you were asked to rate your energy level on a scale of 1 to 10 (low to high), you'd probably have to give it very little actual thought to provide an answer.

Energy's importance in the motivation equation is vast, but it only tells half the story. A high level of energy needs to point towards or away from an action. For this essential element, we look to *direction*.

Direction

The second component of motivation is *direction*. The role of *direction* is to channel and guide energy. Therefore, direction can also be thought of as *steered energy*. As is the case with *energy*, the *direction* is also determined by meanings.

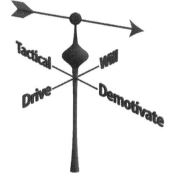

Figure 11 Direction of Motivation

Energy can follow any one of four paths:

1. Will
2. Drive
3. Demotivate
4. Tactical Retreat

Key Learning Points

Motivation is directed energy. Said differently, motivation is a process designed to provide energy and direction based on a like/don't like continuum.

Motivation = Energy + Direction
$$(Mo = E + D)$$

Energy is available power that can vary in intensity. Direction is steered energy.

Energy can be steered to follow any one of four paths

1. Will ("I want to")
2. Drive ("I have to" and "I can't help myself")
3. Demotivate ("I do not want to")
4. Tactical Retreat ("I choose not to")

There are four possible reasons for demotivation:

1. Helpless
2. Apathy
3. Rebellious
4. Distrustful

Components of a Meaningful Ecology

1. Meaningful goals are aspirational ends for good.
2. Meaningful processes are user-friendly approaches that facilitate and allow activities to proceed smoothly.
3. Meaningful settings describe an edifying culture.

Will

People with a willing disposition are attracted to experiences, places, people, and objects because they enjoy them. They do not need to be motivated by external influences because the situation is inherently and intrinsically appealing. Energy-wise, they strive because they are "pulled" by a worthwhile activity and goal. As you can read in Table 5, intrinsically motivated people generally say statements such as "I want to…" "I enjoy…" "I love to…" or "I am passionate about…"

People are voluntarily disposed to engage in activities where they can use their innate strengths and inclinations. For instance, as a rule, a highly social and extroverted person is naturally inclined to seek and interrelate with people. For these extrovert types, jobs and other roles where people interact with others are energizing, so they are more likely to be considered appealing. It might not be so with an introvert who likely would experience spending time with people as energy-depleting. They could do it and even enjoy it. Still, when energy depletion reaches a lower level, they may have to drive and push themselves against their natural inclinations to perform with vitality.

Drive

In MP, the terms [having] *drive* or [being] *driven* do not connote a *willing* motivation, nor do they describe a highly and intrinsically committed individual. Instead, to be *driven* is considered a compulsive and obligatory form of motivation. Important narratives that imply driven behavior include statements such as "I have to…" or "I'm expected to…" as in "I have to feed the family," or "It is my role," "It is my duty," and "I have to be responsible." Of course, to discern if the behavior is genuinely driven, the overall context must be considered. Yet, in our experience, as a rule, such descriptions indicate *driven* behavior.

> "…an unbiased observation of what goes on in man whenever
> he is oriented toward meaning, would reveal the fundamental
> difference between being driven to something, on the one
> hand, and striving for something, on the other hand."
>
> ~ Viktor Frankl ~ [48]

Type	Attitudinal Disposition	Energy Bent	Reward Orientation	Decision
WILL	Attraction	Pull	Intrinsic	"I want to …"
DRIVE	Resistance (Fight)	Push	Extrinsic / Impulsive	"I have to … " "I can't help myself …"
DEMOTIVATE	Avoidance (Flight / Freeze)	Moving away	Extrinsic (Disingenuous) or Intrinsic (Genuine)	"I do not want to …" *Helpless:* "I do not know how to or have what it takes" *Apathy:* "I do not care" *Rebellion:* "I refuse to" *Distrust:* "I don't trust you."
TACTICAL	Avoidance	Willingly Moving Away	Intrinsic	*Prudence:* "I chose not to"

Table 5 Types of Motivation

As a rule, a driven person is busy. Their busyness *could be* productive, but not necessarily so. For instance, management theory speaks of the *activity trap*—where people remain aimlessly busy without knowing why.

> "Activity trap: The **risk of becoming so busy with activity**
> *so as to* **forget and miss the aim of that activity**."

–www.yourdictionary.com– [49]

Because *driven* behavior is compulsive, it has elements of irrationality. A type-A personality, for instance, is a case of a driven person.

> **"Type-A personality:** *A temperament characterized by excessive drive
> and competitiveness, hostility, an unrealistic sense of time urgency,
> inappropriate ambition, a reluctance to provide self-evaluation, a tendency
> to emphasize quantity of output over quality, and a need for control."*

–The Penguin Dictionary of Psychology– [50]

We are not suggesting that all driven actions are of the Type-A personality or are consistently aimless (Activity Trap), but compulsive behavior usually has a distracting, if not disruptive, effect on others and their ability to be fully present and productive.

Just as *will* has its degrees of intensity, so does the *drive* motivation type, and its effect will vary from person to person and from situation to situation. What is familiar to *driven behavior* is that the individual *must* (versus *want to*) act. For instance, an employee who goes to work primarily to "feed the family" is giving a cue for the meaning of why they work. We can infer from the answer that this person cares for their family and is acting responsibly. Without asking more questions, it would be challenging to determine other reasons, usually hidden at an unaware level, why they go to work.

What if that same employee was asked, "If you won a million-dollar lottery prize today, would you continue working here?" and responded that they wouldn't? We could determine from that answer that the individual is *driven* to work. In other words, a version of "I currently do this, but if I had the option, I would not be doing it." A person expressing this sentiment is exhibiting *driven behavior*.

It should be stated that it is possible that removing the need to maintain an income by working (as winning a large sum of money likely would) opens doors to other more exciting possibilities. For instance, when pursuing a much-desired university degree or taking up a passion project. There is the potential that a *stronger will motivation type has replaced a will* motivation type. Each case or situation will have to be evaluated based on conditions.

A person demonstrating *driven* motivation and behavior must overcome the resistance of not wanting to carry out the activity. They must *push* themselves to receive the desired reward (e.g., I work to feed the family) but through unpleasant means. While providing for the family is a meaningful aim, the process of feeding the family in some circumstances can be experienced as a driven, exhausting burden and is, thus, *meaningless*. It becomes meaningless when the drive to work is based on an anxious fear of not providing for the family. Instead, when a willing and confident disposition replaces anxiety, feelings and attention are focused on work and the positive that effort brings. Situations, experiences, people, and objects that require driven motivation will deplete, de-energize, and drain the individual. This sense of exhaustion helps explain why poorly designed jobs and work cultures produce disengaged employees and hence, low productivity. It also explains why some people end their workday feeling "tired" despite carrying out their duties sitting on comfortable chairs.

Demotivated

There are reasons why people distance themselves from engaging in certain activities, going places, and spending time with specific individuals. However, they have one or more unpleasant feelings such as *discomfort, distress, embarrassment, shame, worry, anger, boredom,* and *vulnerability.*

The demotivated individual avoids certain activities because they are considered either difficult, uninspiring, or offensive. Some attributions and figures of speech used to describe an individual with low motivation include "lazy," "lethargic," "procrastinator," "feet-dragger," "indifferent," "conflict-averse," and "insecure." These ascriptions are applied to people who act with intentional slowness, hold back, interrupt, delay, and avoid. These low-energy types of motivation are symptoms of four types of meanings: helpless, apathetic, rebellious, and distrustful.

The Helpless

A person experiences helplessness when they lack the influence or competence to carry out essential tasks. The individual cannot muster internal resources to thrive, adapt, and respond to the demands and expectations set either by their internal standards or external environments. In some way, the helpless individual feels incapacitated, and hence, indisposed to solve pressing problems and engage with others genuinely and effectively. Helplessness can go by different names as well. Other terms that indicate helplessness include *powerless, weak, unfit, incapable, ineffective,* and *impotent.* As a rule, the lack of perceived influence and competence diminishes confidence.

The helpless individual thinks or engages in self-talk using sentiments such as low value or worthlessness, incompetence, inability, and a lack of self-assuredness. Feelings usually associated with a helpless personality include being *sad, depressed, inconsequential, dispirited, foolish, small,* and *insignificant.* The impostor syndrome is a type of helplessness.

There are degrees and types of dependencies, but they are beyond the scope of this book. As a rule, helplessness can result from a lack of competence, meaning (e.g., confidence), or both. Clinically, helplessness can also be a symptom of dependent personality disorder (DPD), defined as *a pervasive dependence on other people.*[51] It is not unusual for some people to feel helpless and frustrated because they do not have the resources and the self-assurance to gain what they want. A goal of MP is to help individuals with helpless symptoms to gain internal confidence, competence, and other resources to achieve meaningful goals.

Apathy

The word *apathy* derives from the Greek *apatheia,* which means "without feeling" or lacking *pathos* or emotion. An apathetic person is generally *indifferent, spiritless, uncaring, disengaged, cold, insensible,* and *impassive.* In addition, apathy can be a form of passive-aggressiveness, depression, exhaustion, not being mindful or careless, being easily distracted, and being fed up.

Apathy can be *genuine* or *disingenuous. Genuine apathy* is a willing and sincere lack of interest in a subject, situation, or person. In genuine apathy, there is no ill intent or desire to minimize another or a situation. For instance, Charlie does not like to watch football games. Charlie has nothing against people who watch football games, the players, the leagues, or sponsors. Instead, Charlie would prefer to spend his time doing something else, something he finds worthwhile.

On the other hand, *disingenuous apathy* does not necessarily mean that the topic or person is sincerely uninteresting. Instead, the individual showing disingenuous apathy *pretends* the subject or person to be unappealing or deserving of her attention. It can be a form of avoidance (e.g., cognitive dissonance), manipulation, disdain, defiance, or rebelliousness. For instance, Mary shares a great idea with her fellow team members, but Sally chooses not to acknowledge and validate Mary's contribution out of envy. Another example could be Peter, who wants to claim ignorance and remain uninformed, so he does not listen to Lucy's evidence. Peter's goal for not listening is to give him a self-devised license to continue following his false narrative.[52]

Apathetic individuals do not demonstrate interest, enthusiasm, or concern for others or situations. In the professional world, they are described as "disengaged" and "actively disengaged." To explain the apathetic state of motivation, people use phrases such as "I don't care," "I am not interested," and "Nothing seems to motivate me."

Apathetic behavior can result from a meaningless task, worldview, or attribution (e.g., an irrelevant or inconsequential action). Logoteleologists (MP practitioners) assist the indifferent individual in determining and committing to a meaningful and intrinsically motivating life task dedicated to benefiting oneself and others.

Rebellious

Rebellion is an attitude fed by fear and anger. It is designed to rebel against, push back, and create distance from unpleasant individuals or circumstances. Energy is channeled to push against (resist) or to separate (move away). Frequently, the goal of a rebellious meaning is to

- Liberate itself from lost freedom
- Avoid being under the control of another
- Seek new and better conditions

A rebellious attitude assumes there is a grievance where a firmly held *belief* or *value* has been or could be violated. As we covered in the first chapter, Beliefs and Values are MTs. Logoteleologists notice how MTs determine the nature and energy of motivation. In some cases, rebelliousness can result from clinical problems, such as an individual with a narcissistic personality.

Words associated with "rebellious" include *seditious, defiant, disobedient, insubordinate, intractable, stubborn, contrarian, traitorous,* and *unruly.* In addition, rebellious individuals take actions such as *pushing (back), fighting, resigning, charging, disputing,* and *disengaging.*

Distrustful

People become distrustful when they sense they cannot rely on others or conditions. Distrust can be due to a lack of control or suspicion of others' intentions. Synonyms of "distrust" include *suspicion, weariness, skepticism,* and *doubt.* Feelings associated with distrust are *disappointment, cynicism, cautiousness,* and *hurt.* Ultimately, distrust leads to distancing or *moving away*—at least—until trust is restored.

Distrust is genuine when the individual follows meaningful guidelines and operates from a sincere desire to reach out and cooperate with others. The goal is to uncover and turn misunderstandings and discrepancies into meaningful solutions. The desire to reach a meaningful answer, in turn, produces a *willing* motivation to succeed with and through others. For instance, Isabel feels unsure about the accuracy of Christopher's (one of her employees) latest financial report. She meets with Christopher to understand and, if required, to improve the accuracy of the work. Her genuine misgiving about the report's content and her commitment to properly support her internal clients yields a document with correct information. Her skepticism is genuine because it is meaningful.

Distrust is disingenuous when the intent is to manipulate at the expense of others (e.g., narcissism). For example, Shawn, a manufacturing product manager, distrusts the logistics function's ability to feed the line with suitable material at the right time to ensure production goals are met. Rather than genuinely sharing his concerns with the logistics staff, Shawn generates rush orders and raises delivery costs to drive the logistics team to meet his goals. What makes this interaction disingenuous is *moving away,* or *disengagement,* from doing what is meaningful (*cooperating*). Instead, cooperation is replaced with a selfish drive (pushing against) to manipulate, harass, and punish.

Tactical Retreat

A person will judiciously disengage from a situation to retreat from the meaningless. It is generally a sign of sound judgment, emotional intelligence, and personal confidence (e.g., self-efficacy). Unlike other disengagement types, a tactical retreat is intrinsic, courageous, well thought out, and discerning. A tactical retreat is not motivated by a desire to avoid confronting a different point of view, nor is it driven by manipulation, fear, anger, or envy. People who practice tactical retreat are honest and unafraid to be wrong or found ignorant. Instead, they disengage to avoid lose-lose outcomes or questionable behavior, situations, and individuals. As a result, they generally will feel self-possessed, calmed, centered, mindful, confident or sure of self, and buoyant. Their response is, for the most part, courteous, respectful, humble, and empathic.

The Motivated Meaningful Meaning Ecology

It is crucial to appreciate the importance of having authentic and meaningful goals, processes, and settings. These three elements are what make up the *Meaningful Meaning Ecology,* as shown in Figure 12. *Meaningful goals* are aspirational ends for good. *Meaningful processes* are user-friendly approaches that facilitate and

Figure 12 Components of a Meaningful Meaning Ecology

allow activities to proceed smoothly. Meaningful processes include supportive decision-making and choice selection guidelines, clear roles, efficient methods, tools, and technologies. *Meaningful settings* describe a culture that meets the Five Meaningful Life Strivings criteria covered in the first chapter (Love, Peace, Happiness, Interest, and Prosperity) and their supportive competencies, *ACT* (Allow, Cooperate, and Transcend). The three components of *ACT* are requisite of the *Meaningful Meaning Ecology*.

A love and passion for what one does, constructive teamwork, and positive and uplifting actions wills motivation to produce meaningful outcomes.

Motivation and Responsibility

Willed or driven individuals who faithfully carry out their duties are many times described as *responsible* and *accountable*. While their attitudes and motives vary, ultimately, the willed or driven performer can deliver results assuming the right competence. However, any perceptive observer can sense the affective and attitudinal difference between *driven* and *willed-inspired* motivation. While not constantly aware, the driven person is more inclined to suffer fatigue and discouragement due to the draining effect of propelling the action. Simultaneously, the genuinely willed individual is energized by the task and so experiences a state of flow.

> *Flow: "A state in which people are so involved in an activity that nothing else seems to matter; the experience is so enjoyable that people will continue to do it even at great cost, for the sheer sake of doing it."*

> *– Csikszentmihalyi –* [53]

A will-motivated individual controls their own inner experience and masters their fate. A driven-motivated individual, in turn, is pushed by unseen forces outside of their control. Finally, compared to a will-disposed counterpart, the driven person is more prone to derail professionally or spoil relationships.

What Triggers Motivation?

Motivation is triggered by a wave of instructions from the meaning-set known as a *telosponse* (See Figure 13, below). [54] The telosponse is the handoff between the meaning-construct or system and the motivation-construct or system to

- Ascribe the energy level
- Assign a type of direction (Will, Drive, Demotivate, Tactical Retreat)
- Fulfill the meaning

Figure 13 Telosponse

It can also be said that a telosponse is

- The transition point between meaning and motivation
- The moment a meaning becomes a determined motive
- The beginning of motivation
- A point of mobilization
- A decision point
- A choice
- A point of no return

> *"To devise a human teleology we require a concept based on final (which includes formal) causation."*

"A telosponse is the affirmation or taking of a position regarding meaningful content … relating to a referent acting as a purpose for the sake of which behavior is then intended. Affirmation encompasses predication."

> *"We must understand telosponsivity exclusively from an introspective perspective in which meaning extends as behavior unfolds." "If there is no meaning involved, then there is no telosponsivity involved."*

~ *Joseph F. Rychlack* ~ [55]

Our motivation's quality and staying power are intimately related to the strength and vigor of our meanings. A meaningful and robust meaning *wills* and *retreats tactically*. In turn, a meaningless and dissonant meaning yields *driven* and *demotivated* energy.

As illustrated in Figure 14, the LIMA is a cyclical flow of energy that starts with meaning and ends with *feedback* where the

- *Telosponse* (Gr. *Telos* = Purpose) determines energy and direction for action
- *Thelosponse* (Gr. *Thelos* = Will) a volley of impulses that fuel a response or action
- *Drásisponse* (Gr. *Drási* = action) activity and a spur to respond
- *Apórroiasponse* (Gr. *Apórroia* = aftereffect) an impact with a consequence
- *Anádrasisponse* (Gr. *Anádrasi* = feedback) the consequence is channeled and received for decoding to determine if there is a match between meaning intent and consequence

The LIMA is a self-regulation system that acts like a Global Positioning System (GPS). The self-regulation system is designed to fulfill meanings. This logoteleological GPS is fueled by motivation and self-corrects until the meaning aim is achieved.

> *"My point is that whether you experience positivity or not depends vitally on how you think. Positive emotions—like all emotions— arise from how you interpret events and ideas as they unfold"*
>
> ~ *Barbara L. Frederickson* ~ [56]

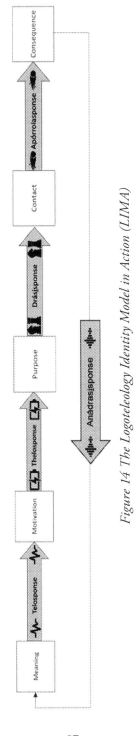

Figure 14 The Logoteleology Identity Model in Action (LIMA)

How MP Improves Motivation

Logoteleologists assist clients in countering the dispiriting effect of driven and demotivated behavior through confidence-building meanings and competencies. Motivation (or the lack of it) applies to individuals, groups, organizations, communities, and even nations. As we have stated, the quality of motivation is a direct outcome of meaning and the meaning-set's quality. Remember that it is meanings that determine the type and strength of motivation.

"For action to occur we need additional intentions…"

"Precisely how many additional intentions…depends on their value for the person, from which the action-intention draws its motivation (based on positive or negative affective assessments)."

~ Joseph F. Rychlack ~ [57]

Identifying the content and dynamics of a meaning-set—Attributes, Beliefs, Values, Feelings, Attitudes, and Aims—allows Logoteleologists to discern how the client interprets the situation and how to best respond. The Logoteleologist helps clients

- Become aware of hidden meanings
- See the connection between the meaning they give to the situation and the type and strength of their motivation
- Explore and select meaningful options that will trigger a confident and willing disposition

Motivation, too, can be frustrated when, despite the best meaning-intentions, the individual lacks the knowledge, skills, preferences, innate strengths, and inclinations to succeed. For instance, the inability to translate meaning-aims into purposeful action could be due to a lack of competence (e.g., a person who cannot repair his car's engine). The man might have the best of meaning-intentions to solve the problem but is not trained to diagnose and fix it. He will have to call upon someone trained and capable, and equipped to solve the particular issue. "I want" (meaning-aim) does not always mean "I can" (Purposeful-action). To bring about a result, one must know *how to*.

In addition to competencies, people are motivated to engage in specific tasks and activities following natural strengths, preferences, and inclinations. For example, consider how some people prefer to write with their left hand while others are inclined toward their right. Whatever the tendency is, it comes naturally, makes things more manageable, and operates on autopilot.

These preferences are valuable because they can help individuals discover a career and vocational path that they are well suited to (e.g., find and do what gives meaning to their life). Logical types, for instance, are more inclined to be rational and may work well in fields such as accounting and engineering. On the other hand, intuitive-subjective type personalities feel more at home working in vocations where feelings, rather than things, play a central role, such as in the social sciences. Someone introverted is naturally inclined to be more comfortable spending time alone than one who is extroverted, so they may flourish, compared to an extrovert, in a field requiring some isolation. Hence, natural strengths, preferences, and inclinations within the meaning-set also influence the type and intensity of motivation.

The MP theory and method support building robust and resilient meanings and the will to succeed. Also, the method

- Supports clients in discovering their innate strengths
- Develops skills that are compatible with their meanings and vocation

Apply MP!

Boosting your knowledge and skills, in effect improving upon your strengths, has a direct and energizing positive impact on motivation. Knowing *how* to engage translates to a heightened ability to bring your *why* to action. Seeking to improve your understanding by taking these steps will raise the odds that your efforts will hit their most meaningful mark.

Chapter Summary and Review

Motivation can be studied and as a construct and as a process. To explain the construct, we use the formula, *Motivation = Energy + Direction*. As a process, motivation is tasked to fuel purposeful action following an attitudinal direction in a like-don't like continuum. Hence, motivation is directive energy.

Direction, the second element in the motivation-construct, steers energy in one of four ways: will, drive, demotivate, and tactical retreat. Will is intrinsic and pulled by a goal. On the other hand, a person's drive is influenced by extrinsic meanings. Driven effort presses or pushes toward the goal. A person invests energy, either will or drive, to get the job done. However, driven motivation is generally impulsive and excessive. Demotivated denotes low energy and an avoidance stance. Demotivation can be extrinsic or intrinsic, as ruled by conditions. Four mental states cause demotivation: helplessness, apathy, rebelliousness, and distrust. A tactical retreat is intrinsically willed to avoid meaningless situations.

We believe three elements promote an engaged and willing disposition: meaningful goals, processes, and settings. Goals are aspirational ends for good. Processes facilitate the accomplishment of goals. Finally, meaningful environments comply with the Five Meaningful Life Strivings requisites and their corresponding competencies, Allow, Cooperate, and Transcend (ACT).

Meanings trigger motivation through a telosponse: the handoff by the meaning-set to motivation through a wave of instructions.

Our motivations' quality and staying power are intimately related to the strength and vigor of our meanings. Meaningful meanings generate a willing disposition, be it to pull or to retreat tactically. Conversely, meaningless meanings stimulate driven and demotivated energy.

The Logoteleology Identity Model in Action or LIMA illustrates how the flow of energy starts and ends at the meaning-set. Understanding the LIMA allows Logoteleologists to appreciate how the quality of meanings and purpose determine the level of motivation invested. MP helps improve people's motivation by enhancing the quality of their meanings (i.e., causes) and purpose (i.e., competencies).

Reflection and Practice

1. Think about one or two work activities you like doing:
    a. What makes the activity appealing to you?
    b. Do you have the right skills to do it well?
    c. Does performing the duty come naturally to you? Why and how?
    d. What type of motivation best describes how you experience carrying out this task?
2. Think about one or two work activities you dislike:
    a. What makes the activity unappealing?
    b. Do you have the right skills to perform the activity well?
    c. Does performing this duty come naturally to you? Why? How does it feel?
    d. What type of motivation best describes performing this task?
3. How could these motivation types, and levels of energy, explain engagement and commitment within organizations?
4. What could be done differently to improve motivation? How can meaningfulness play a role?

Chapter Five

Blocks to Meaning

"Any fool can know. The point is to understand."

~ *Albert Einstein* ~ [58]

"It is sobering to think that you and I can know about a social process that distorts our thinking and still be susceptible to it."

~ *David G. Myers, Ph.D., Hope College* ~ [59]

What if we could conquer the enemy of success and human thriving? Why don't we learn from the lessons of history and continue to repeat the mistakes of the past? Why do some people resist truth and seem to operate out of reality? Is there a way to understand why and how—as a species—we resist what is good for us? This chapter will address these and similar questions.

After reading this chapter, you will be able to…

- Understand and describe how meanings determine a worldview
- Detect what prevents self-awareness
- Explain why problems remain unresolved despite solutions being available
- Recognize and determine how self-awareness and meaningful thriving can be improved

Mankind…does not suffer from a lack of answers. Rather, it suffers despite the answers being available.

How do meanings determine a worldview?

Chapter Two explained how five meaning antecedents form meanings:

1. Our biogenetic DNA
2. Family (psychosocial) influence
3. Culture (sociocultural) or following dominant social norms
4. Accumulated learning and life experiences (biographic history)
5. Current situation and context

These antecedents form our worldview: a mental model of reality, lodged in our default personal meaning DNA or *meaning of life* (a subject we will expand on in Chapter Six). As explained in Chapter One, this default meaning DNA holds information in a meaning-set (Attributes, Beliefs, Values, Feelings, Attitudes, and Aims) employed to explain the self, the world, and how the world works (i.e., worldview).

> *Worldview: "a particular philosophy of life or conception of the world."*
>
> *~ Microsoft Bing Online Dictionary ~* [60]

A worldview is a double edge sword. On the one hand, a worldview provides predictability. It allows people to adapt and function in their environments and to respond to situations. For instance, it enables the individual to follow cultural, social, legal, spiritual, and family norms and traditions. But, on the other hand, different worldviews challenge our comfort zone and lead to misunderstandings and even conflict.

Blocks to Meaning Awareness

The obstacles to awareness are readily available in psychological literature. Related theories inclde:

- Self-justification
- Cognitive dissonance
- Repression
- Resistance

Key Learning Points

Meaning Antecedents form our worldview: a mental model of reality lodged in our default personal meaning DNA or meaning of life. A worldview is a double edge sword. On the one hand, a worldview provides predictability. While on the other hand, they can also lead to cognitive dissonance and even conflict.

Logoteleologists are not only attentive to phenomena concerning the unconscious ability to perceive, but they are also mainly concerned with how—despite being fully aware—data is avoided, distorted, reinterpreted, or refused.

The inability, refusal, or apathy to perceive and to respond to sensible incoming data we call meaning-calcification.

Meaning-calcification (i.e., blockage of flawed meanings) gives rise to meaning-sclerosis—the absence of critical information for sound judgment, success, and thriving.

Biased meaning-sets are calcified by faulty and meaningless meaning antecedents.

The logoteleologist helps the client to become aware and to understand what the meaning of the block is (e.g., why the resistance), its purpose (e.g., what the client does), and how it is experienced (e.g., consequence). One approach to expose and replace meaning blocks is through a meaning-set analysis.

- Projections
- Blind spots
- Impostor syndrome
- Confirmation bias
- Attribution error
- Attentional allocation
- Psychophysiological phenomena
- Escalation to Commitment
- Other coping and ego-defense mechanisms

Our intent is not to rehash these readily available explanations. Instead, since our approach is logoteleological meaningfully or goal-oriented, we use the terms *meaning-calcification* and *meaning-sclerosis* to explain and treat blocks to meaning.

Many factors can limit perception, some operating at the unaware level, such as blind spots and conditioning effects. These are difficult to perceive unless brought to our consciousness by others or circumstances. We cannot be aware of what we cannot perceive, so we cannot respond appropriately. For our purposes, we seek to answer the questions,

- Why and when do we not perceive?
- Why once made aware, does the person block information?

Consider a logoteleological explanation as to *why* a person becomes overtly or covertly defensive. When someone hears negative feedback they may know that they tend to resist this kind of critique. Why might this happen? What triggers such defensiveness? Logoteleologists are not only attentive to phenomena concerning the unconscious ability to perceive. They are also concerned with how (despite being fully aware) data is avoided, distorted, reinterpreted, or refused. That is where meaning-calcification and meaning-sclerosis come in.

Meaning-calcification

The dictionary defines calcification as *a hardening or solidifying; rigidity*.[61] It is natural for humans to filter incoming information.[62] Being rooted in meaning can be viewed as a positive state. However, such a fixed disposition can also lead to inflexibility and even stubbornness when contradicted. This inability, refusal, or antipathy to perceive and respond to sensible incoming data we call meaning-*calcification*. It is the outcome of a psychological ossification of one or more meanings. Meaning-calcification explains how a meaning-set's[63] content[64] is programmed to lock out some incoming information. Similar to other schools of psychology,[65] Logoteleologists help clients understand how mental processes block perception and penetrating insight (e. g. understanding consequence and resistance to feedback).

Have you ever wondered why some people resist unbiased truth? Why would anyone object to reason, diverse perspectives, indisputable evidence, and proven common sense? It can be said, using computer language, that the flawed meaning-set has a "virus" or "bug," preventing self-awareness (e.g., blind spots). An applicable acronym that explains the phenomenon is GI-GO, which stands for Garbage In—Garbage Out. A flawed meaning-set can be unreasonable.

> *"Nobody adopts antisocial behaviour unless they fear that*
> *they will fail if they remain on the social side of life."*
>
> *~ Alfred Adler ~* [66]

Sources of meaning-calcification are varied, and many, some referenced above, are already covered in psychology literature. Calcification symptoms come across as confusion, ignorance, apathy, stubbornness, cynicism, and defensiveness. It defines a sidetracked or flawed mindset and a worldview determined to avoid, filter, and obstruct incoming information.

However, it must be said that not all mental blocks are ill-intended or pursue an antagonistic goal. For instance, a person can hold a worldview and comfort zone conditioned by cultural upbringing. Feeling out of place when operating in a diverse setting is reasonable. Assuming an open mind, understanding, adapting, and aptly engaging in unfamiliar environments can take time.

Nevertheless, at its worst, meaning-calcification operates as an evil demon who will not relinquish its hold on its victim and requires expert remedial support. Thus, while Logoteleologists treat meaning-calcification, the emphasis of the discipline lies in prevention by helping individuals, families, groups, organizations, and nations form healthy (meaningful) worldview meanings (i.e., the meaning of life). The goal is to transition from false and unprincipled meanings to meanings that are true and moral.

"It is easier to fight for one's principles than to live up to them."

~ Alfred Adler ~ [67]

What is the source of meaning-calcification?

From early life, meaning antecedents form our worldviews and influence how we perceive and respond to situations. The quality of meaning antecedents determines how open and receptive we are to possibilities, diversity, tolerance, respect, curiosity, and change. Healthy meaning antecedents can lead to intellectual curiosity, honesty, transparency, and *meaningful* behavior.

On the other hand, biased meaning-sets are calcified by incomplete, faulty, and meaningless meaning antecedents. We all have *incomplete meaning-sets,* and so all hold some level and kind of bias. Recall from the section on identity that individuals have unique meaning antecedents, such as a combination of culture, language, family, and regional differences. It is these shared social meanings that determine our comfort zones. Hence, it is reasonable to feel odd or standing out in foreign or different settings.

In contrast, *faulty and meaningless meanings* lack curiosity and tolerance. Flawed and meaningless intentions can produce disapproving behavior driven by fear, distrust, and ignorance. While it requires a measure of self-awareness and analysis, there is good news here. We can improve the content of our meanings to live a meaningful and prosperous life.

It is essential to understand meaning-calcification and its consequences. Calcified meanings lack intelligence and health. Hence, these types of meanings can produce grim outcomes. They are particularly dangerous when the meaning type value is unintelligent, weak, and corrupt. Knowingly accepting, endorsing, conspiring with, and acting out a corrupt intent is possibly the most dangerous act a human being can commit. The following section, meaning-sclerosis, will explain why and how.

"A lie would have no sense unless the truth were felt as dangerous."

~ Alfred Adler ~ [68]

Meaning-sclerosis

Meaning-calcification (i.e., obstructive meaning) gives rise to *meaning-sclerosis*, the absence of critical information for sound judgment, success, and thriving. Hence, meaning-sclerosis is a state, indication, and even a warning of ignorant and unhealthy meanings.

Meaning-calcification inhibits insight. Low insight produces meaning-sclerosis or inhibited judgment.

For instance, bias (i.e., meaning-calcification) prevents objective listening and making sound decisions (meaning-sclerosis). Logoteleologists help clients avoid and reduce meaning-calcification to eliminate meaning-sclerosis (a harmful effect or consequence). The goal is to replace meaningless meanings with meaningful meanings. The replacement process includes revealing and analyzing the usefulness and relevance of meaning antecedent content.

The improvement process requires improving the intelligence and health of the whole meaning, emphasizing values, the mental storehouse of ethics, and the human conscience.

Apply MP: Tackling Meaning-calcification and Meaning-sclerosis

If we accept the premise that meaning antecedents shape the content of our meanings and hence our worldview, improvement starts with *exploring how and why we block information*. Obstacles are in place for a reason, generally to protect us from a real, flawed, or fictional threat. The meaningful purpose psychology (MP) method helps the client to

- Become more self-aware
- Understand the meaning of the obstacles (i.e., why the resistance)
- Know the purpose of the barriers (i.e., through what the client does)
- Evaluate the consequence of the obstruction (i.e., how self and others experience it)
- Explore meaningful options
- Replace the old (flawed) meanings with new ones
- Build meaning intelligence and health

"If you can't avoid a situation that brings you needless negativity, you have at least three options for curbing it: you can modify the situation, you can attend to different aspects of the situation, or you can change its meaning."

~ Barbara L. Frederickson ~ [69]

Consider the example of two siblings arguing about whose turn it is to do the dishes. A third party (e.g., mom) mediating to determine who will do the dishes today and who will do them tomorrow might be fair and reasonable.

Nevertheless, this common-sense solution does not address why the siblings could not follow a civil and sensible (meaningful) approach to agree and why instead, they resorted to arguing. In this situation, each pursued a self-orientation instead of responding to each other's needs. Negative attributions and differing values at the meaning type-level could contribute to the blockage. The attributions and the lack of shared values are symptoms of meaning-calcification, which appear as an argument. The siblings' inability to decide who is going to do the dishes portrays a meaning-sclerosis. Again, meaning-calcification is the cause of meaning-sclerosis.

MP has multiple methods to deal with flawed meanings. One mentioned includes exploring and analyzing the content of the meaning-set and its quality. Leveraging the six MTs, here are some sample questions we could ask to increase awareness and explain what is happening:

1. Attributions:
    a. What are the motives of your opponents?
    b. What labels would you use to describe those who disagree with you?

    c.   Why do you think they disagree with you? What is their intention?

2.   Beliefs:

    a.   What evidence justifies blocking incoming information?

    b.   What reasons do you use to explain why you do not want or care to listen to a different point of view?

    c.   What is your "truth," and what is the other party's "truth"? What is the contrast?

3.   Values:

    a.   Is there an agreement or contract between the parties involved in the situation to rule decision-making?

    b.   Are you operating from a moral or ethical standard? If so, which?

    c.   Do you have shared expectations?

4.   Feelings:

    a.   What feelings do your opponents provoke in you?

    b.   How do you feel when a sensitive subject comes up?

    c.   What do you feel when others do not support your views, conclusions, and choices?

    d.   What do you feel when you discover you were wrong?

5.   Attitudes:

    a.   How important is it for you to win the argument?

    b.   How disposed are you to listen to someone who has a different perspective, belief, or value system? Why?

    c.   Are you willing to change when proven wrong?

6.   Aims:

    a.   What conclusions lead you to resist information?

    b.   What is the object of resisting?

    c.   What decision have you made?

Low Meaning Congruence and Consequences

Considering your answers to the previous questions, to what degree is there alignment and congruence among all MTs? What could be the consequence of a lack of agreement? Logoteleologists inquire and encourage the client to pay attention to these inner voices or self-talk to discern agreement. It is essential to understand how the agreement or lack of alignment among the MTs explains consequence; and what to do about it.

> *"Men of genius are admired, men of wealth are envied, men of power are feared; but only men of character are trusted."*
>
> ~ *Alfred Adler* ~ [70]

Chapter Summary and Review

The source of our worldview, our conception of the world, lies in the content of meaning antecedents. Meaning antecedents shape our philosophy or meaning of life. Meaning antecedents include our biological DNA, the influence of family, society and culture, our life experiences, and current context and situation. Meaning antecedents help us adapt and thrive in familiar environments and conditions, but they can also challenge us in unfamiliar territory.

Flawed meaning antecedents create imperfect meanings. As previously stated, a faulty meaning can be calcified or hardened. A calcified meaning prevents data from getting through. Just as blood cannot flow through hardened veins without difficulty, information cannot flow unbiased through calcified meaning-sets.

Meaning-calcification leads to meaning-sclerosis.

One approach to help clients remove meaning-calcification from their meaning-sets is by exploring the content and aim of the blockage. The logoteleologist asks questions to provoke insightful answers that can, in turn, lead to practical solutions. One approach to expose flawed meaning-set content is asking questions using the MTs: Attributes, Beliefs, Values, Feelings, Attitudes, and Aims.

The goal is to:

- Remove the calcification or blocks to meaning
- Replace flawed meanings with better options
- Promote greater openness and flow of information
- Enhance sound and meaningful judgment

Reflection and Practice

1. What is your worldview or philosophy of life?
2. How happy or pleased are you with your worldview or philosophy of life?
3. What shaped your worldview (recall the five meaning antecedents)?
4. What are the strengths, potential flaws, and risks of your worldview?
5. How do you block your self-awareness? How would those who know you well describe how you prevent or avoid uncomfortable situations?
6. Leveraging the six MTs (meaning-construct), what questions would you ask yourself to understand why and how you block information?

Chapter Six

Meaning of Life and Meaning in Life

"…he allowed himself to be swayed by his conviction that human beings are not born once and for all on the day their mothers give birth to them, but that life obliges them over and over again to give birth to themselves."

~ Gabriel García Márquez, *Love in the Time of Cholera* ~ [71]

Do you have and guide your life by a clear, confident, and goal-oriented meaning of life? What makes life worth living? How can a plan in life help a person and others succeed?

After reading this chapter, you will be able to…

- Understand meaningful purpose psychology's (MP) framework for *meaning of life* and *meaning in life*
- Recognize and explain the contrast between *meaning of life* and *meaning in life*
- Realize how *meaning of life* and *meaning in life*, while different, are both relevant

MP's Framework for a Meaning of Life

The concept of the *meaning of life* is likely not new to any of us. It has been pondered for ages and is often regarded as external, even universal. Something that has been determined by someone else and applies to all humans in the same way. Like an answer to be discovered, a treasure to be found, or the solution to a riddle.

Logoteleologists understand and explain the existential concept of *meaning of life* from an identity perspective. To do this, even to comprehend the meaning of life notion, we must first return to the topic of Identity that we covered back in Chapter Three. From the Three Identity Types section, professors Peter J. Burke and Jan E. Stets[72] established three identities: role, social (group), and person. Briefly explained again within the added context of a meaning of life, they are

1. **Role identity.** "A role is the set of *expectations* tied to a social position that guide people's attitudes and behaviors."[73] Being part of a group, such as a family, a social club, or a sports team, for instance, entails meeting expectations. People meet such expectations through duties and responsibilities. Just as a business organization might have a "job description" to list goals, it informs and guides employees to carry out tasks. The "skills and qualifications requirements" part of the job description tells us whether the applicant will have the ability to meet the role's expectations.

   For instance, the role of an author requires publishing articles and books. Therefore, the author (as role-incumbent) must be competent in critical thinking, outlining, and writing coherently to publish. In turn, for an elder sibling in a family, the role expectation could include babysitting younger brothers and sisters. To be a caretaker, skills such as changing diapers, protecting, nurturing, consoling, and playing are required.

   Concerning this family role, the role identity would be used to answer, "What is expected of me as a member of this family, and of the specific role I hold?" The position within the family indicates the value the person brings. The role identity determines any expectations that other family members might have about what is required within the role (e.g., parents' expectations of a child).

2. **Social Identity.** "A social identity is based on a person's identification with a social group. A social group is a set of individuals who share

the view that they are members of the same social category."[74] For example, being British has a social identity that is different from the Angolan social identity. It describes inter-group phenomena such as "in-group versus out-group" and "us versus them." Social identities include nationality, family clan, gender, race, religion, social status, political affiliation, and membership in professional and academic organizations. These social identity categories bring people together and may also set them apart from other groups of people. Consider what categorizations you have that align you within a group. What do you have in common with other members of those groups, and what makes you a good fit? Are there any downsides to being a part of the group? For example, does being a part of a particular group create a barrier or divide between you and members of a different group? Understanding our own social identities can come from answering these questions and others like them.

Having a social identity, or holding membership in a group, entails adding value through the role identity. Hence, there is a price of admission (e.g., expectation) and a cost of retention (through role identity fulfillment) that comes with belonging. In addition, belonging to a group entails acting consistently with principles such as loyalty and contributing a valuable service to the group's explicit and implicit mission and goals. Finally, belonging also involves having authority, responsibility, and accountability to the group.

3. **Person identity.** "The *person identity* is the set of meanings that define the person as a unique individual rather than as a role-holder or group member."[75] Person identity is what differentiates each human being from others. The previously mentioned meaning antecedents shape this identity.

As psychological beings, we humans share common mental processes. Yet each of us is unique because of our "meaning imprint"—the meanings we give to our unique identity that cannot be duplicated. [76]

An identity has much to do with a person's meaning of life.

Each person's identity is different and unique and cannot be replicated. Think of how your life experience is different from others. Your view of the world is unique. Your presence on this planet is historically, psychologically, and physically distinct, exceptional, and irreplaceable. In other words, you are positively extraordinary. Your distinct and unique identity with all its potentiality cannot be duplicated. Fortunately, because you are unique, you are not expected by life to be an impersonator, or worse, an impostor. This is what makes human life priceless, the fact that no person can take another's place or fulfill the duty that life asks of him or her to fulfill. Think abut it: there is and will only be one model of each human being—past, present, and future. There is only one you. What you are called to do by life no one else can do in your stead. [77]

This information related to meaning antecedents shaping identity and identities' role in meaning of life is introduced and discussed in further detail in The Path to a Meaningful Purpose.

Notice in the previous paragraph that the keywords related to identity are "distinct" and "unique." Observe also that the content alludes to that each person is irreplaceable. You were born with a person, role, and social identities. Through these three identities, life placed explicit and implicit expectations on your being.

Hence, your life has a default meaning (i.e., to meet the expectations set by life) requiring purpose-related skills and competencies.

Said differently, each human being is born with a default person, social, and role descriptions and specifications (i.e., the required competencies to succeed in life). To fulfill such requirements, people must be dependable and responsible. Also, to succeed in life, the expectations must be clear and understood. People cannot succeed in life when expectations are unknown, vague, and flawed. Perfect or imperfect, these default person, social, and role descriptions carry the person's meaning of life psychological instructions. Finally, to fulfill the requirements, people need to equip themselves with the appropriate skills and abilities to fulfill life's demands and opportunities.

Key Learning Points

According to Burke and Stets, there are three identities: role, social, and person.

Meaning of life is the active fulfillment of a personal mission. It answers the sample question, "Why do I live?" The meaning of life explains the reason or the goal of life.

All human beings are born with a default meaning of life. The default person, social and role descriptions are meanings, and they carry the person's meaning of life psychological instructions (i.e., scripts).

A default meaning of life starts at the time of conception (biogenetically) and remains operating on (subconscious) autopilot to influence behavior through life until it is self-determined.

A default meaning of life can be meaningful and meaningless, and determined by the quality of meaning antecedents.

A self-determined meaning of life entails freely choosing one's identity and life mission.

While the meaning of life is about identities and pursuing a personal life goal, meaning in life is about what the individual finds to be motivating and gratifying. Hence, meaning in life describes what a person finds to be fulfilling.

What is the Meaning of Life?

Meaning of life is *the active fulfillment of a personal mission*. It answers the sample question, "Why do I live?" The logoteleological answer to "Why do I live?" is simple: "You live to do what you are doing now." Our behavior mirrors our meanings. The meaning type Aims expresses a personal mission. As will be covered below, all human beings are born with a default meaning of life.

This purposeful pursuit of the fulfillment of one's personal mission can serve as a compass to inform decisions in all that they do. We all have a meaning of life that we operate with daily, but this does not necessarily happen consciously. We believe that most people are not aware of or in touch with their operating meaning of life. However, the LIMA model and process can help us access and assess the content and mission of our default meaning of life.

Two Types of Meaning of Life

There are two types of *meaning of life*: default and self-determined.

1. **Default Meaning of Life**. Every child is born with an identity. It can be said that the newborn had no say or option to select their name, parents, family economic circumstances and status, nationality, race, and biological DNA. In other words, the newborn's family, social, and biogenetic antecedents were preselected for the child by others and circumstances. Based on Burke and Stets's identity model, the child is born with a default role, social, and person identities.

    Also, innate at birth is *potential: the latent qualities and abilities to develop and to achieve*. Under the right conditions (i.e., the meaningful path), this potential is released for good and even greatness. However, under the wrong circumstances (i.e., the meaningless path), the child's potential can be hindered and even corrupted. Thus, the quality of meaning antecedents largely determines these paths.

"Life is like a game of cards. The hand you are dealt is determinism; the way you play is free will."

~ Jawaharlal Nehru ~ [78]

Hence, there are three ways to define a default meaning of life:

a. **Life-goals**. These goals are established at birth and fulfilled through identities (role, social, and person).

b. **Meaning antecedents.** These meaning precursors determine personality life scripts. A life script's subconscious goal establishes what a person will do with their life—a goal that is not self-determined.[79]

c. **A prescribed worldview and a person's role and mission in it**. Here, the individual has been preconditioned (e.g., through *introjections* and *socialization*) to provide predictable preordained responses to life's demands and expectations without fully knowing why (e.g., introjected regulation).

Introjection: "an unconscious psychic process by which a person incorporates into his or her own psychic apparatus the characteristics of another person or object."

~www.thefreedictionary.com~ [80]

"'Introjected regulation' refers to the process of being directed by internal prod and pressures such as self-esteem-relevant contingencies. When a regulation has been introjected, it is internal to the person in the sense that the behavior no longer requires overtly external prompts, but the regulation process motivating is still external to the self. Introjected regulation, then, describes a form of internalized motivation in which actions are controlled by intrapsychic, esteem related contingencies. Thus, such actions are also said to have an external perceived locus of causality."

~Ryan, et al.~ [81]

All three have in common the predestined meanings given to self, others, and situations, which are fulfilled by actions fueled by motivation.

A default meaning of life starts at the time of conception (biogenetically). After that, it operates on autopilot—a psychological control system that automatically maintains a preset meaning-determined heading (e.g., logoteleological)—through life.

"Adler's goal concept is characterized particularly by the fact that the individual is largely unaware of his goal, that it is a hidden or unconscious goal, a goal which the individual does not understand. It is the true nature of the individual's hidden goal which constitutes according to Adler, the essential content of the unconscious."

~ Ansbacher & Ansbacher ~ [82]

The default meaning of life remains active, for good or for bad, until its content is exposed, analyzed, and either:

a. validated and kept as helpful (no action required.)
b. reinforced and enhanced in its meaningful foundation (boost its impact.)
c. improved where lacking (clarify, refine, and repair.)
d. replaced by another better version (substitute identity elements with more promising and genuine meaningful meanings.)

2. **Self-determined Meaning of Life.** A self-determined individual follows convictions and behavior unaffected by extrinsic or external forces. Hence, a self-determined meaning of life entails freely choosing one's identity and life mission.

Worth repeating, a self-determined meaning of life entails:

  a. Becoming aware of the current default operating meaning of life

  b. Analyzing the quality of the current default operating meaning of life (where *meaningful edification* is the quality standard)

  c. Validating the current default operating meaning of life (i.e., no changes are required)

  d. Replacing the default meaning of life with a more meaningful self-determined option

  e. Building on the self-determined meaningful meaning of life (i.e., enhancing, elevating, or transcending its positive impact through edification)

  f. Improving or polishing the self-determined meaning of life (i.e., selective clarification, improvement, refinement, and replacement)

  g. Persevering, sustaining, and perpetuating the new and genuine identity

Key Learning Points

Meaningful purpose psychology (MP) encourages people to determine their own fate through a meaningful meaning of life. A meaning of life without external compulsion, and freely claimed and asserted. All roles too should have a self-determined meaning that are aligned and supportive of the meaning of life. For instance, what is the meaning of being in the role of a spouse?

There are four elements in a meaningful meaning of life statement:

1. What is the title of the role you play? (e.g., farmer, manufacturer, family, father, mother, son, leader, manager, CFO, etc.)
2. What do you do, or will you do? (Your purpose.)
3. For whom? (Who benefits from what you do?)
4. For what benefit? (What meaningful meaning will you accomplish?)

A meaningful role purpose applies to one person, a group, a company, a nation, as well as an international community.

In MP theory, the standard to analyze, modify, and improve a meaning of life is through

- meaningful beliefs and values
- natural attributes

We stated that the meaning of life is *the active fulfillment of a personal mission.* It answers the sample question, "Why do I live?" This particular mission is fulfilled through person, social, and role identities. As such, the *meaning of life explains the reason or the goal of life.*

If the meaning of life is about fulfilling a mission, how does it differ from *meaning in ife*?

Meaningful Purpose Psychology's Framework and Definition for a Meaning in Life

> *"To the degree that individuals have attained a sense of self, they can act in accord or be 'true' to that self."*
>
> ~ *Richard M. Ryan and Edward L. Deci* ~ [83]

While the *meaning of life* is about identities and fulfilling a personal life goal, *meaning in life* describes what the individual finds to be motivating and gratifying.[84] For example, an ideal meaning in life experience would include Mihaly Csikszentmihalyi's definition of *Flow:*

> *"…the state in which people are so involved in an activity that nothing else seems to matter; the experience itself is so enjoyable that people will do it even at great cost, for the sheer sake of doing it."*
>
> *~Csikszentmihalyi~* [85]

Key Learning Points

Meaning in life is not always benign. A meaning in life can fall in any given point within a meaningless/meaningful range or scale.

The path to a successful existence is through a self-determined meaningful meaning in life. Your meaning of life should be self-determined and powered by what makes life intrinsically worth living (i.e., your meaning in life).

Pursuing meaningful ends is about engaging in edifying activities for self, others, and the environment.

The default meaning of life remains active—for good or for bad—until its content is exposed, analyzed, and either:

a. validated and kept as helpful (no action required.)
b. reinforced and enhanced in its meaningful foundation (boost its impact.)
c. improved where lacking (clarify, refine, and repair.)
d. replaced by another better version (substitute elements of the identity with more promising and genuine meaningful meanings.)

In short, having meaning in life is what makes life fulfilling and worth living.

However, meaning in life is not always benign. A meaning in life can fall at any given point within a meaningless/meaningful range or scale.[86] On the one hand, unfortunately, some people find meaning by engaging in worthless or meaningless activities, such as bullying others, drug and alcohol abuse, selfish thoughts and actions, and committing crimes. On the other hand, some find their meaning in life by leveraging their inherent talents and strengths for noble and meaningful ends

These generous and consequential ends include being sensible, respectful, responsible, and compassionate. In addition, it can be expressed through creative and innovative acts, such as in the arts, entertainment, and architecture. In sum, pursuing meaningful ends is about engaging in edifying activities for self, others, and the environment.

Meaning in life answers the sample questions,

- "What intrinsically motivates me?"
- "What am I generally curious about?"
- "What activities of my choosing give meaning (significance) to my life?"
- "What do I enjoy doing?"

A Congruent Meaning of Life and Meaning in Life

We explained that the meaning of life is tied to an identity, a default identity with implicit and prearranged expectations we did not choose, and actively influences our worldview and behavior throughout life. We also explained that while this default identity has been imposed on us, it can be analyzed, validated, modified, and improved. The goal of this discerning process is to:

- Self-determine who we are
- Decide the direction for a path forward

But what criteria should we use to analyze our default meaning of life? And when we state "analyzed, validated, modified, and improved," what standard should we follow?

Standard to Analyze, Validate, Modify, and Improve the Meaning of Life

In MP theory, we use two standards from the meaning-set content:

- Meaningful beliefs and values
- Natural attributes

Meaningful Beliefs and Values

As covered previously in Chapter Two, meaningful beliefs and values are fulfilled through the *Five Meaningful Life Strivings* standard:[87]

- Love
- Peace and peace of mind
- Happiness
- Engagement/Interest
- Prosperity

These five criteria are used to determine how well beliefs and values fit a meaningful standard. If it is determined that there are factors not in alignment (e.g., beliefs and values that prioritize prosperity above all else) they must be modified. The modification enables harmony with the meaning of life. Another way to think of this is as promoting a more *meaningful* meaning of life.

Natural Attributes

In MP, natural attributes are likings, inclinations, talents, and strengths inherent in every human being.

- **Likings** are activities we enjoy doing. As an example, some people enjoy gardening.
- **Inclinations** are natural attributes that make doing things easy for us. Humans tend to be inclined toward activities they find comfortable and natural to do (likings). For instance, a person with extroverted tendencies will naturally seek and enjoy being with people. At the

same time, an introvert might be actively social but will get to a point desiring solitude and quiet time, at least more than the extrovert might.

- **Talents** are built through skill practice and experience. As a rule, people develop talents doing things that come easy to them (inclinations) and which they enjoy (likings). A case in point is a violinist who practices at least five hours a day until she masters her instrument and impresses her listeners.
- **Strengths** are a collection of talents. An example of strength is a baseball player's ability to pitch well, bat above average, frequently steal a base, and inspire team members to cooperate.

The standard to analyze, modify, and improve the meaning of life is through meaningful beliefs and values (i.e., Meaningful Life Strivings) and making the best of our natural attributes.

Keep in mind that Beliefs, Values, and Attributes are meaning types.

Competencies

Our ability to accomplish and even exceed the expectations of our meanings require competent and skilled purposeful actions. To succeed, we must embrace a life-long vocation to improve our talents through study and practice.

Apply MP!

Making the Most of Meaning of Life

To self-determine and optimize one's meaning of life, one must

- Embrace the standards of a meaningful life
- Discover and leverage natural attributes
- Do what gives life meaning (meaning in life)
- Build the skills to achieve

The path to a successful existence is through a self-determined meaning in life, as long as the meaning in life is meaningful and edifying. Therefore, your meaning of life should be self-determined and powered by what makes life intrinsically worth living (your meaning in life).

Chapter Summary and Review

Humans are innately born with three identities: *role, social, and person*. All three come with a "job description" that includes duties and responsibilities and the ability and behavioral requirements to succeed and belong.

Role identity is a position within a group identity: sibling, manager, CEO, and parent.

A *social identity* is a unique group category comprised of members who share and are committed to a joint mission. This mission can be explicit or implicit. Social identity entails having members who contribute to the group mission through their role identities. Examples of social identities include family, clans, citizens, race, religion, nation, alliances, and political orientation.

Person identity describes the distinguishing and unique physical and mental attributes of an individual. Person identity distinguishes an individual from others.

The three identities justify answering the question, "I am_____."

The three identities' expectations (i.e., duties and responsibilities) represent a person's *meaning of life*. In meaningful purpose psychology (MP), the *meaning of life* is the active fulfillment of the expectations set by the tasks demanded by life through our roles, social memberships, and personality. The *tasks demanded by life* are the expectations we have of others and ourselves, others have of us, or circumstances require. These duties require acting responsibly and being accountable. For instance, we are expected to pay taxes to benefit our respective countries and communities' shared social identity as citizens. To succeed successfully at these tasks, we need knowledge, skills, and abilities.

There are two types of meaning of life: *default* and *self-determined*. We are born into default role, social, and person identities. We do not have a say regarding our name, skin color, language, nationality, parents, siblings, rank, and social standing from conception. A self-determined meaning of life is freely chosen.

Meaning in life explains what makes life fulfilling and worth living. A meaning in life can be benign and happy or meaningless. A fulfilling and worth living life follows *the path to a meaningful purpose*:

1. Sharing experience with loving people
2. Living in peace and having peace of mind
3. Experiencing a state of contentment and joy
4. Doing interesting things with interesting people in interesting places
5. Progressing intellectually, experientially, and financially. Creating a worthwhile legacy.

A meaningful life requires we do what we enjoy leveraging our natural attributes, talents, and strengths. The MP method was conceived to create institutions (social identities) to fulfill meaning in life through their role and person identities. The MP approach also helps people develop and align their self-determined meaning of life with, and in support of, their meaningful meaning of life.

Reflection and Practice

1. Ponder on your default meaning of life. You have been living as if what is your meaning of life?
2. In what ways have you self-determined who you are and what you do with your life?
3. What is going well, and what could be improved in your meaning of life?
4. What gives your life meaning (as in meaning in life)? What are your natural attributes?
5. How could you leverage what gives your life meaning to help you self-determine your meaning of life?
6. How and why are the meaningful meaning of life and meaningful role purpose helpful?
7. Write a preliminary draft of your meaningful meaning of life. Refine over time.

Chapter Seven

The AVR Method©

"First, learn the meaning of what you say, and then speak."

~ Epictetus ~ [88]

After reading this chapter, you will be able to…

- Define and apply the AVR Method©
- Explain the goal of the AVR Method©
- Outline and define the stages of the AVR Method©
- Recognize when and how certified Logoteleologists use this method

What is the AVR Method©?

The AVR Method© is a foundational logoteleological procedure used to help individuals, groups, organizations, and even nations to examine and (when required) improve their meanings. Other MP models supplement and complement the AVR Method©. The approach has application in therapy, coaching, counseling, consulting, and development. In a nutshell, the AVR Method© helps clients live a meaningful life by increasing meaning intelligence, health, and accuracy.

What is the Goal of the AVR Method©?

The AVR Method© helps the individual live a meaningful life by:

- Allowing unobstructed access to their meanings
- Increasing intrapersonal and interpersonal meaning accuracy and congruence
- Removing meaningless obstacles and distractions
- Adding and strengthening meaningful meanings to thrive in life
- Improving the ability to discover, and make the most of, what gives life meaning (i.e., meaning in life)
- Equipping individuals with improved ability to claim a self-determined meaning of life

We will first explain the concept of gaining unobstructed access to meanings, followed by meaning accuracy and later by meaning congruence.

Accessing Meanings

We covered in *Chapter Five: Blocks to Meaning*, that:

- Meanings determine our worldview
- A meaning-construct can become calcified and thus block awareness and resolution
- Meaning-calcification frustrates the free flow of information, leading to meaning-sclerosis
- The way to reduce the effect of meaning-sclerosis is to remove the blocks to meaning (i.e., meaning-calcification)
- The client is encouraged to give priority to confronting the blocks within the meaning-set

Having access to relevant internal and external information is perhaps one of the most significant challenges humanity confronts. Unfortunately, we are bound to filter out consequential data types based on blind spots and biases. Just as we can select a TV or radio channel to exclude others, the mind too can tune in to a specific wavelength at the exclusion of other media with their respective sources of information. However, the channels are available *if* we choose to access the meaningful ones. The Logoteleologist's task in accessing meanings is to help the client broaden their reception band to be appropriately informed, achieve meaning accuracy, and exercise free will effectively (i.e., meaning intelligence and health).

Achieving Meaning Accuracy

In meaningful purpose psychology (MP), *the meaningful* is the standard to determine and increase meaning accuracy and reduce meaning discrepancy. Let's recall from Chapter Two that *the meaningful:*

- is positive, mutually beneficial, transcendental, altruistic, virtuous, and replenishing
- has five components in its construct: *The Five Meaningful Life Strivings* or the innate human aspirations of *Love, Peace, Happiness, Interest,* and *Prosperity*
- is conveyed through three key core competencies, Allow, Cooperate, and Transcend (ACT)

Being meaningful is being kind to one's self (intrapersonal), as well as to others (interpersonal).

It must be said that there is such a thing as *meaningless meaning accuracy,* where a corrupt meaning-set can effectively harm oneself and others. This option has already been shown to counter human thriving. [89] For more information on *meaningless meaning accuracy,* as well as the broader topic of *meaningful* versus *meaningless,* you can review *Chapter Two: What is Meaningful and Important.*

Achieving Intrapersonal Meaning Accuracy

The Merriam-Webster Dictionary defines accuracy as

- "Conformity to truth or to a standard or model: exactness"
- "Degree of conformity of a measure to a standard or a true value" [90]

As we have discussed, the value or standard worth following is meaningful meanings (Love, Peace, Happiness, Interest, and Prosperity) and their respective meaningful-consistent behaviors. Hence, following meaningful meanings and behaviors is compatible with a meaningful life. Intrapersonal meaning accuracy engenders self-confidence, faithfulness, serenity (i.e., being centered), predictability, and stability with important things in life. Individuals with reliable and accurate intrapersonal meaningful meanings know what they stand for (i.e., self-determination) and are confident concerning their meaningful meaning in life and purpose (i.e., self-evaluation: "Am I on target?").

Achieving Interpersonal Meaning Accuracy

To attain interpersonal meaning accuracy, two or more people must agree upon and share the meanings and approaches. The two components that are necessary for this shared meaning agreement are compatibility and mutuality. Compatibility, defined [91] as "a state in which two things can exist or occur together without problems or conflict," and "a feeling of sympathy and friendship; like-mindedness," is critical because the lack of this element (as seen in the definition) leads to conflict. Compatibility within the meaning-sets of two or more people leads to harmony and allows for the second necessary component for achieving interpersonal meaning accuracy, mutuality.

Mutual is defined as "held in common by two or more parties," and mutuality as "the sharing of a feeling, action, or relationship between two or more parties." [92] These definitions show that there needs to be a shared connection between parties for something to be mutual. Moreover, as the concept of mutuality relates to the respective meaning-set content of those involved (i.e., interpersonal), it requires that they are shared, similar, and (remember) compatible. Said differently, all parties' meanings are in harmony as they agree, align, and follow the same aims and standards.

In summary, interpersonal meaning accuracy entails getting along with others without cruel unprincipled conflict (and thus harmoniously) to fulfill a shared goal. Moreover, the group members' meaning-set content is like-minded and hence compatible.

"If a relationship is incompatible, it is because its members are incongruous *(they do not 'mesh' or 'fit together'),* discordant *(they are 'out of harmony' or 'out of sync' with each other), or* disagreeing *(they do not share common attitudes, goals, feelings, etc.). By implication, if a relationship is compatible, it is because its members are* congruous *(they do 'mesh together'),* accordant *(they are 'in harmony' or 'in sync' with each other), or* agreeing *(they share common attitudes, goals, feelings, etc.)"*

~ William Ikes ~ [93]

Logoteleologists study and assess the quality of both *intrapersonal* and *interpersonal accuracy* through the Logoteleology Identity Model (LIM) and the meaning-construct. The MP (logoteleology) goal is to strengthen meaning discrepancy-reducing processes and capabilities or said differently to increase meaning accuracy capability for what is meaningful.

Achieving Meaning Congruence

Meaning accuracy requires a congruent meaning-set. The Merriam-Webster Dictionary [94] defines congruence as "the quality or state of agreeing, coinciding, or being congruent." Within a meaning-set, congruence is obtained when all MTs agree, cooperate, and follow-through. Thus, the state of congruence is necessary to achieve an aim accurately. Yet, it must not be assumed that all MTs always concur and comply within a meaning-set. For instance, it is not uncommon for individuals to have conflicting beliefs (e.g., cognitive dissonance, paradox, dilemma) that undermine the will to act meaningfully, even when the outcomes would benefit all concerned. For more information, review *Chapter Five: Blocks to Meaning.*

The degree of congruence in a meaning-set regulates motivational certainty, confidence, and determination. Conversely, low congruence leads to intrapersonal and interpersonal dissonance, paradox, and conflict, increasing the odds of symptoms such as stress, anxiety, inadequacy, and guilt.

A congruent meaning-set contains harmonious MTs. In other words, there is rapport, agreement, compatibility, and consonance among the six MTs.

Examples of Intrapersonal Congruent and Incongruent Meaning-sets

The following example is of the experience of a professional named Paul, who is considering approaching his leader for a raise.

Paul has been working for Funkie Standards for three years. While he has been a good performer, his yearly raises are not at par with industry rates. As a result, he is considering asking his boss for a fair raise. But, first, let's examine potential congruent and incongruent narratives that may apply to Paul's situation by meaning type.

Meaning Type	Congruent Narratives	Incongruent Narratives
Attitudes	Inclined to confront his leader.	Reluctant to confront his leader.
Attributions	About self: I am and have been a good performer. About the manager: He is a fair-minded person.	About self: I am and have been a good performer. About the manager: I am not sure he is a fair-minded person.
Feelings	Optimistic and confident	Scared and unsure.
Beliefs	I should be paid according to industry standards. If we cannot agree, I can always find another job elsewhere.	I should be paid according to industry standards. But what if the boss disagrees? Will I embarrass myself?
Values	People should be paid fairly.	People should be paid fairly, but the boss should not be contradicted.
Aims	I will set an appointment with my manager today to ask for a raise.	I am not sure I want to confront them or I may be better leaving it alone.

Table 6 Meaning Type Congruent and Incongruent Narratives

Reducing Meaning Discrepancy and Incongruence

In the congruent or harmonious narratives, all six MTs are in sync to meet the challenge. On the other hand, the column with the incongruent descriptions explains why Paul aims "I am not sure I want to confront them or I may be better leaving it alone." Incongruent narratives can have both positive and negative MTs competing against or overwhelming other types. For instance, Paul's values are overridden by other MTs. Congruent meaning-set narratives increase the odds for meaning accuracy. Logoteleologists help reduce intrapersonal and interpersonal meaning discord through the AVR Method©. They do so by increasing meaning accuracy.

What are the stages and definitions of the AVR Method©?

The AVR Method© helps clients grow through the assistance of certified and licensed MP coaches, consultants, counselors, or therapists. AVR stands for meaning awareness, analysis, validation, re-decision, replacement and realignment, reintegration, and reinforcement/sustainment. The method improves meaningful meaning accuracy.

1. **Meaning Awareness** entails bringing to one's attention what is not known, perceived, and understood. [95] To be aware is to make contact with ourselves and perceive our surroundings. It is about being conscious of what we give attention to and not. Awareness determines how in tune we are with the self and with others. To be aware is to know.

2. **Meaning Analysis** involves helping the client understand the "so what" or the implications, impact, and consequence of the meaning given to self, others, and situations.

3. **Meaning Validation** tests the quality of the meaning given to self, others, and situations (i.e., intelligent and healthy meanings). The MP gold standard is *Meaningfulness*. [96]

4. **Meaning Re-decision** quizzes the client's readiness to confront reality and commit to improving

Key Learning Points

The AVR Method© is the fundamental logoteleological procedure designed to help individuals, groups, organizations, and even nations to examine and—when required—improve their meanings.

The AVR Method© follows seven phases. Meaning…

1. Awareness
2. Analysis
3. Validation
4. Re-decision
5. Replacement and Realignment
6. Reintegration
7. Reinforcement/Sustainment

The goal of the AVR Method© is to help the person live a meaningful life by

- gaining unobstructed access to their meanings
- increasing intrapersonal and interpersonal meaning accuracy and congruence
- reducing intrapersonal and interpersonal meaning discrepancy and incongruence and hence removing meaningless obstacles and distractions

In MP, the standard to determine and to increase meaning accuracy and reducing meaning discrepancy is the "meaningful."

The AVR Method© is usually complemented by the Logoteleology Identity Model and the meaning-set (construct), applicable to all four practices (i.e., therapy, coaching, consulting, and counseling)

5. **Meaning Replacement and Realignment** is where meaningless meanings are replaced, realigned, improved, enhanced, and finetuned with meaningful options. The goal of this phase is to
   a. improve the quality of meaning-content
   b. ensure such content within the meaning-set is harmonious and coherent
   c. identify, learn, and practice complementary and fitting skills in a safe setting

6. **Meaning Reintegration** entails identifying targets of opportunity within the client's context to act meaningfully. The client is encouraged to *renew, reconcile, and reinvigorate* relationships. While the previous step identifies, plans, and practices improvements, *reintegration* requires:
   a. applying new patterns for relating with others
   b. implementing skills to gain access to one's and others' meanings, and for noble ends
   c. constructing with stakeholders a mutually meaningful compatible reality.

7. **Meaning Reinforcement or Sustainment** is the improvement phase where success is celebrated, reinforced, and sustained. This phase requires building a support system to aid the improvements over time.

How do Certified Logoteleologists use the AVR Method©?

The AVR Method© has application in MP and can be customized for therapists, counselors, coaches, and consultants. All four customized approaches are complemented with the Logoteleology Identity Model (LIM, discussed in Chapter Three) and the meaning-construct (covered in Chapter One).

Here we will offer general guidelines and tips to benefit all types of practitioners.

Key Learning Points

Individuals with dependable and accurate intrapersonal meaningful meanings know what they stand for (i.e., self-determination) and where they stand concerning their meaningful meaning of life (i.e., self-evaluation: "Am I on target?").

There is such a thing as *meaningless meaning accuracy*, where a corrupt meaning-set can seek to harm self and others.

Accuracy is defined as

- "conformity to truth or to a standard or model: exactness"
- "degree of conformity of a measure to a standard or a true value"

Compatibility is defined as

- "a state in which two things can exist or occur together without problems or conflict."
- "a feeling of sympathy and friendship; like-mindedness."

A goal of the practitioner is to help the client harmonize his or her meaning-set with meaningful content. In other words, there is rapport, agreement, compatibility, and consonance among the six MTs.

A meaningful harmonious meaning-set exhibits a healthy individual, group, and community (local, national, and international).

For Human Thriving

MP posits that there are solutions to human problems. We believe that most social problems are self-inflicted. We also believe that humanity can discover what truly matters in life, and by exercising their free will, can select meaningful options to thrive in life. We feel confident that the path to a meaningful purpose leads to success in life. That path requires that we:

- Care for one another
- Promote peace and peace of mind
- Foster conditions where people live happily
- Engage in exciting activities with interesting people in interesting places, and for noble ends
- Prosper intellectually, experientially, and financially

The AVR Method© helps people

- Discover what gives meaning to life (i.e., meaning in life)
- Claim their meaning of life

The Client-Practitioner Contract

All responsible and ethical work between clients and practitioners should clarify goals, roles, processes, and norms upfront. It is helpful to have a standard contract for your private practice. Also, the practitioner should be aware of and comply with any local, state, and federal standards about the helping professions, including having insurance coverage. Getting legal advice is encouraged.

While not a comprehensive list, here are some ideas worth considering when you contract with clients:

1. **Goal**. Determine what the purpose of the working relationship is. Focus on desired outcomes. For instance, encouraging the client to write a goal such as, "By the end of the process, I will be able to successfully...." As the client becomes aware of new opportunities, they can make updates.

2. **Measuring success**. Agree on tangible measures for success. For instance, it could be becoming more aware, forecasting the consequence of various options, and consistently selecting the right choice. It could also include learning and becoming more skillful. For a workgroup or organization, the measure could be improving profit by 10%. It is valuable to use psychometrics and feedback from others for pre and post-assessment.

3. **Role clarification**. This entails clarifying expectations. For an Organization Development (OD) practitioner, it could involve not practicing surrogate leadership or doing proxy work on behalf of the client. The axiom is that OD consultants consult, and leader-clients lead. For a coach, for instance, it could entail explaining that practitioners facilitate and, as a rule, do not provide answers. Practitioners are encouraged to follow additional role guidelines for their particular fields.

4. **Norms**. The client and practitioner should clarify what information is and is not confidential and who can access it. The practitioner should also be upfront about fees and when payments are due. It can also include arriving on time to sessions and doing homework and any cancellation policy costs. Other norms can be negotiated over time as required.

5. **Methods**. Include information about the process and what the client must do to make the most of the experience. This information should incorporate the length of each session and the overall developmental program. It could also involve the practitioner interviewing other stakeholders, using questionnaires and other valuable tools to gather relevant information.

These steps are more than a client-agreement arrangement. The process should mirror how two responsible adults manage a successful relationship. The method's learning process entails practicing an ideal client-coach relationship. The learning supports the meaning replacement, reintegration, and sustainment phases of the AVR Method©.

The AVR Method© and Logoteleology
Identity Model in Action (LIMA)

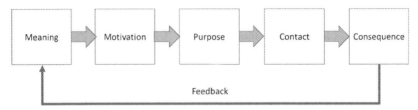

Figure 15 The Logoteleology Identity Model in Action (LIMA)

As mentioned previously (Chapter Three), practitioners use the identity model for intrapersonal or intragroup awareness, analysis, validation, and improvement. Again, through targeted questions, the practitioner can start the improvement process from any of the five components. Here are some examples:

Meaning

- What was your original goal or intention?
- What was or is your operating meaning of "marriage"?
- Why would you intend to discipline your students that way?
- What did you assume your boss would say?
- How were you feeling when considering your options?

The MP practitioner uses the MTs of the meaning-set construct to inform the questions they ask. Suggestions are made later in the chapter.

Motivation

- How committed are you to do this?
- Are you submitting to your partner's wishes?
- I notice hesitation. Am I reading you right?
- I hear you say that you work long hours, and time at work prevents you from experiencing a healthy work-life balance. Using the

motivation model (from Chapter Four), how would you categorize your motivation?

- There seems to be a consensus in your 360° feedback that you tend to procrastinate. What feeds that indecision?

Motivation questions are intended to bring awareness to meaningful meanings and promote the desire to act upon them. For instance, there could be a positive meaning intent, and yet, due to the lack of skills, the individual is incapable of achieving the desired results.

Motivation questions are very similar to those asked by the meaning type *Attitudes*. Therefore, the attitude in the meaning-construct plays a significant role in determining the type of motivation.

Purpose in Action

- What skills or competencies are required to succeed?
- What did you do?
- What did you tell your manager? How did you answer her?
- Explain to me your plans to bring this solution to life.
- If I was a fly on the wall, what would I see you doing and saying?

Remember, purpose questions pertain to the field of skills, competence, and activities. The goal of purpose is to fulfill meanings.

Contact

- How did your spouse receive your response?
- Did you feel welcomed by the group?
- What is her perspective on the situation?
- Why was he so upset?
- What is important to him?

Consequence

- Did you achieve the results you expected?
- What meaning have you given to your life in its current state?
- What was the outcome of your actions?
- What do these outcomes say about the quality of your meanings, motivation, and purpose? What is the overall story?
- If you wish to experience something different, what needs to change? Why?

Asking consequence-type questions will point to the model's previous three elements' contributions, thus clarifying the situation.

Feedback

- How did she respond?
- What did you hear from the team?
- How do you respond to feedback?
- How do you remain informed?
- How do you know the impact you are having on others?
- Do you ask for feedback?

A competent practitioner asks questions to help the client be more self-aware and to navigate smoothly through the stages of the AVR Method©.

The AVR Method© and the Logoteleology Meaning-construct

As discussed in *Chapter One: What is Meaning,* meaningful purpose psychology (MP) practitioners use the meaning (types) construct to help the client navigate through the stages of the AVR Method©. The goal is to inquire using the meaning-construct and following the steps of the AVR Model©. This approach will help the client:

- Be more self-aware
- Analyze the impact (consequence) of the meanings

- Assess the quality of their identity using the Logoteleology Identity Model (LIM)
- Discover how they prevent themselves from succeeding and why
- Determine the level of commitment to improve
- Replace meaningless meanings with more healthy options
- Practice and build abilities in a safe setting
- Repair relationships and build robust social networks and communities
- Improve the quality of motivation
- Thrive!

Here are examples of meaning-set construct questions and statements a practitioner could use.

Attributions

- Why would he do that to the team?
- How do your employees perceive you? What would they attribute to being accurate about you?
- Based on how you self-describe, what opinion do you hold about yourself?
- How does this attribution explain your attitude and feelings toward her?
- What intent are you attributing to the politicians from the other party?

Beliefs

- What happened?
- What is her version of "the truth"?
- What are the facts?
- Do you have an opinion or hunch as to why this happened?
- Whose role is it to shut the valves at the end of the day?
- Is this a conservative or a progressive position?

Values

- What are your values regarding how others must be treated?
- What moral or ethical standard was violated?
- Explain to me what you two agreed to do?
- What guidelines influence how you run and succeed in your marriage?
- Does this team have explicit, evident, and shared values and norms on how to get things done successfully?

Feelings

- How are you feeling now?
- What did you feel when he walked away?
- If I heard someone say that to me, I think I would be upset and angry.
- I am sorry you had to experience so much pain, but there is hope.
- How did you feel when you finally got your hard-earned diploma?

Attitudes

- How would your boss and peers describe your attitude toward report writing?
- Did you like it or not?
- What made it so attractive that you would pursue it?
- Why are spiders so disgusting to you?
- What are you generally inclined to enjoy doing at work, and what do you typically avoid?
- On a scale of one (low) to ten (high), how likely are you to repeat this?

Aims

- What do you aim to do?
- What have you concluded is the path to follow?
- How will this potential choice help you and others?
- How well-founded is your conclusion?
- When will I see you again?

Now we'll take a look at what the AVR method© looks like in action by using a real example from a coaching session facilitated by Luis A. Marrero, one of the coauthors of this book. The name of the client and any other potentially identifying information have been edited to ensure anonymity.

AVR Process: Phillip's Case Study

Phillip sought coaching because he had a temper problem. As he described his issue, Phillip became angry when he could not get his way and have others decide and act as he thought they should. His temper was affecting his reputation at work. Phillip fears how he handles conflict could lead to him losing his job. His moods also interfere with his interactions with others in his personal life, resulting in an inability to maintain a steady romantic relationship, for example.

Human Resources and his supervisor had made Philip aware that he needed to change his attitude, but he did not know how to control himself. While he had tried multiple approaches, he was still unsuccessful. Finally, after hearing about the effectiveness of the MP approach, he came to me for help.

While I will explain Phillip's situation following the AVR Process steps, it is essential to remember that it is iterative and not always sequential. In the conversation that follows, you'll see that Phillip progresses through the different stages of the AVR Method©. As this unfolds, there is at several points the need to circle back to reinforce the earlier stages as new information emerges. This reinforcement is a natural part of the coaching process and an essential step to solidify understanding and assimilation going forward. It is not uncommon for the individual or group being coached, Phillip in the example that follows, to avoid or resist information. This information ends up becoming the blocks to meaning that lead to the consequences being experienced. It is up to the coach to discern, call out, and challenge when they notice this resistance. This awareness and intervention is where the growth happens.

Additionally, in the conversation with Phillip, you'll see there are parenthetical notations at points along the way. The purpose of these important notes is twofold. First, they call out where certain logoteleological concepts come into play when working through the AVR Method©. This highlighting enables tying the steps in the process back to the concepts of MP as seen in real-time. Second, they provide valuable insight into the experienced logoteleology practitioner's internal thoughts as the client provides or responds to information. These notes allow you, the reader, to not just observe the interaction of a proper coaching session but to sit in the coach's seat as it plays out.

Coaching Session # 1

Meaning Awareness

During the first phase of the process, my goal was to help Phillip thoroughly understand his situation. In other words, we would invest time understanding his anger and what provoked it. I leveraged the Logoteleology Identity Model (LIM) and meaning-construct to help him be more aware of himself, the situation, context, and other people involved.

Luis (Coach): Tell me, Phillip, when you get angry, what do you do? (Purposeful Action)

Phillip (Coachee): In some way or another, I go on the offensive. I raise my voice and tell people what to do and how to do it. What I believe to be the correct way or what I want. If they object or push back, I tend to insist. I have difficulty backing down. I am either very convinced of what I want and believe and won't back down or have a problem acknowledging I am wrong.

Luis: You go on the offensive, raise your voice, tell people what to do and how. You push back to any counter-argument or reason they might provide. Acknowledging you are wrong is difficult for you. Did I understand you?

Phillip: Yes, you did.

Luis: Do you raise your voice initially, or do you progress on your volume and intensity?

Phillip: Good observation. I firmly state my opinion or what I want and then raise my voice and tone if I find the other party resisting me.

Luis: So, as you remember, you tend to talk first and then increase the volume of your voice as you become frustrated when others do not hear what you are saying and resist.

Phillip: That is correct.

Luis: Phillip, is anger the only feeling you sense, or are there other feelings present? (Feeling Meaning Type [MT])

Phillip: I never thought of it; what I feel, I mean. So what do I feel? Anxiety, definitely. Upset, anger, and resentment.

Luis: Where do you feel them in your body?

Phillip: In my head. Sometimes in my shoulders. Also, the area around my stomach.

Luis: Of those physical areas, which one stands out?

Phillip: Probably my stomach area. Why? Why does where I sense my feelings matter?

Luis: In logoteleology science, feelings mean something. Knowing what and where you feel can help detect what the feelings mean and how they shape outcomes. Sometimes feelings can take us to good places, and sometimes they do not. This intentional awareness of one's feelings and what they want can help you better handle them to ensure positive outcomes.

Part of our work is to help you be mindful and attentive to what you feel and think. The more alert and aware you become of what is happening in your body, the better your ability to deliver an on-target response.

Phillip: I never imagined thinking about feelings in that way. That's interesting and intriguing.

Luis: In my experience, I learned that many people are not fully aware of their feelings and what they mean. You are not alone. We will cover the subject more thoroughly as we continue our work.

Ready to go on?

Phillip: Yes.

Luis: You shared that when upset, you most feel it in your stomach. Describe to me what your stomach experiences.

Phillip: Well, there is a tension, a tightening in my gut.

Luis: What else? Think of situations where you have felt angry. What else do you feel?

Phillip: I feel anxious. The anxiety moves from my stomach to my head, where I feel pressure. Actually, my upper body becomes tense.

Luis: So, your anger is most apparent in the area of your gut, then you feel a tension in your head too, and finally the upper part of your body? Does that feel like the sequence?

Phillip: Yes. That is what happens.

Luis: Phillip, I would like to invite you to be attentive to your physical upsets and any other significant feeling—both out there and here with me. The goal is for you to be more mindful, noticing what you feel and where.

Would you be willing to share feelings in these coaching sessions?

I would also like to encourage you to journal when you experience these angry episodes and capture what you feel and where. Would you be willing to do that?

Phillip: I am not the type who talks much about my feelings; this is one of those few occasions I have done so. But I can give it a try.

Luis: (Luis makes a mental note that Phillip is not the type to share his feelings with others but defers to address it another time.) I would like you not to try but rather do. Would you be willing to commit to sharing your feelings rather than just agree to try to do it?

Phillip: I see what you mean. Okay, I will do the journal assignment and share my feelings with you.

Luis: Great! We will go slowly to build your comfort in sharing and exploring your feelings. (Luis makes a mental note that one of the ways Phillip might prevent himself from improving is by being disconnected from his feelings.)

Here are some tips to stay connected with your feelings. First, remember that sensing means something. What I am encouraging you to do is to pay attention to them. For example, when you feel the tension on your stomach, your head, and shoulders, remember they are telling you something. Based on what you are sharing, these feelings drive motivation or energy in action to fuel your response. As we continue our work, you will learn additional steps to explore your feelings. For now, I encourage you to notice the tension and other associated feelings. Just be more aware of them. Deal?

Phillip: Deal.

Meaning Analysis

Luis: We have been on the subject of feelings. I want to make a shift in understanding how your actions impact others. My question to you is: How do people respond when you direct your anger to them? (this speaks to the consequence, an aspect of the Logoteleology Identity Model in Action [LIMA]).

Phillip: It depends on who it is and the situation. It varies from people either distancing from me to confronting me. (Attitude MT)

Luis: Let us then start with those who report to you. How do they respond when you get angry?

Phillip: Most listen and remain quiet. One or two will explain why, or justify the adverse outcomes and suggest we learn from the experience, and move on.

Luis: Do you listen empathically to their version of the situation?

Phillip: Empathically, no. Remember, they are not doing their job. That is why I get upset.

Luis: Can I safely assume that you do not listen or believe their side of the story?

Phillip: Luis, the reason I get upset is that the problem keeps happening. That is why I get angry at them.

Luis: How do you think they feel towards you and the situation?

Phillip: Towards me, probably frustrated and intimidated. That is what my 360-degree feedback states and what I heard from my Human Resources (HR) representative and my boss. So that is why I am talking to you today.

Luis: Can we agree then that when you become angry with your team members, you raise your voice and do not listen empathically? (Purposeful Action)

Phillip: That is what happens when they fail.

Luis: As a result, some of your team members remain quiet; others give their side of the story and even propose to learn from the failure? (Consequence)

Phillip: Yes.

Luis: And your leader and HR rep are telling you that the team feels frustrated and intimidated? (Consequence)

Phillip: Yes.

Luis: Do you agree your behavior frustrates and intimidates others? (Luis is testing to see if Phillip takes responsibility for how others feel when he gets angry at them.)

Phillip: Well, the feedback is undeniable. I don't know how to respond differently, Luis. I have high standards and feel exposed when my team fails me.

Luis: Having high standards speaks well of you, Phillip. We will come back to your standards later. (Values MT) And about how to respond differently, that is why we are here. I am sure that with your commitment to the coaching process, you will be able to improve.

I am now attempting to understand if you are ready to validate how people feel when you get angry and accept responsibility for your impact on others.

Meaning Validation

Phillip: Yes, I know I frustrate and intimidate others (consequence). And there is a part of me that feels guilty and ashamed for it; and that I need a coach to improve myself. However, I look forward to learning not to cause the team to feel this way but still have them achieve the expected business outcomes.

Luis: Accepting responsibility for the impact you have on others is a good step. Without it, one cannot improve. So I congratulate you for your courage to accept responsibility and for sharing with me how you feel.

Philip: (Phillip nods positively and yet somber.)

You shared that you feel guilty and ashamed. Referring to the meaning-construct, I shared with you previously, what value or standard of conduct was violated that made you feel guilty and ashamed? (Values MT)

Phillip: I feel bad that other people feel bad because of me.

Luis: I understand. Yet, what I am probing is about a value, standard, and expectation you have, that when you violate it, it leads to your feelings or remorse. Think "10 Commandments" type language. As in "You will or will not so-and-so."

Phillip: I guess "you should not make people feel bad."

Luis: Why? Why is it wrong to make people feel bad? Tell me what is behind this value or standard?

Phillip: Well, being insensitive and hurting others is not okay.

Luis: Phillip, does it have to do with how people deserve to be treated, and moreover, how they do not deserve to be treated? (Values MT)

Phillip: Yes, definitely. No one ever asked me about my values before, nor did I think about them as I am doing now with you.

Luis: In my practice and experience, Phillip, many people are unaware of the values that are compelling their behavior. These are also referred to as their operating values. Through my involvement working with people, not many have thought about knowing and understanding how they self-regulate through values. I discovered that many people have not even validated the quality of their life and professional standards to make choices and decisions. This absence of values awareness and guidance happens at all levels: governments, business organizations, families, communities, and even religious organizations. I also believe that one of the main reasons humanity has so many problems is the absence of values and practicing self-defeating and corrupt morals.

I propose that—among other areas of improvement, through this coaching process—you bring to your awareness, examine and validate the quality of your values to build confidence in doing what produces genuine happiness, prosperity, and success in life.

Meaning Re-decision

Luis: Is this something you are willing to examine and improve where it makes sense?

Phillip: Yes. I want to continue moving forward. There is a lot I have to process. You have asked questions and proposed alternatives I never considered. This process is beneficial, but I am mentally tired.

Luis: This might be an excellent place to stop today's coaching session. Let's first talk about what would be beneficial to do between today's session and our next meeting:

- We agreed you would journal about when you feel angry and what provokes it.
- Also, Phillip, pay attention to your feelings and their role in how you respond and how others react to you.
- I would also like to invite you to read my articles about MTs, specifically those explaining what is meaningful and important in life and the identity formula. Then, when we get back together, we will discuss the content and review how the concepts can help you.
- Finally, let me encourage you to journal a description of your value system, mainly as it shows up and could be when you relate to your reports. What is for you, good or bad, and right and wrong, and why? As with the feelings assignments, this reflection on values should be an iterative process.

I will follow up on this assignment through email. Is that a deal?

Phillip: Definitely! Thanks!

Coaching Session # 2

(The first part of the coaching session was invested in ensuring Phillip understood the meaning-construct, what makes life meaningful, and the Logoteleology Identity Model (LIM). The reader can refer to chapters one through three of this book.)

Luis: Now that you have a handle on relevant aspects of the MP theory, Phillip, tell me about your assignment on paying attention to your feelings. How did it go?

Phillip: I never thought of pausing to experience in the moment what I was feeling. It is a brand new experience. In addition to the journal, I wrote the word "feel" on a sticky note to remind me to notice what I was feeling. I attach it to my work documents to have it before me as I interact with others.

Luis: What did you experience?

Phillip: Well, I was more aware of my emotional reactions.

Luis: Your impulses?

Phillip: Yes, what I felt. It allowed me to notice and stop myself from responding the way I usually respond. Your article on what makes a meaning meaningful was helpful. I set a goal of getting my point across without offending others.

Luis: You deliberately attempted to have a better, positive, and meaningful consequence rather than responding in meaningless ways. (consequence)

Phillip: That is correct!

Luis: How did the articles help you select meaningful options?

Phillip: Using the meaning-construct, I noticed that I was making negative attributions about staff members and violated my values on how people deserve to be treated.

Yet, Luis, what about the value that we must deliver quality service and product?

Luis: Are both noble? Specifically, treating people respectfully and delivering a quality service and product?

Phillip: Of course.

Luis: Do these values contradict themselves? Is it possible to treat people with respect and deliver quality service and products?

Phillip: It should be. Then why don't they do the right thing? Why can't I attribute that they are lazy or resisting me when they are not delivering the expected results?

Luis: Good question. Why are they not doing the right thing? What do they need to know and do to succeed? Have you considered their belief meaning type, the storehouse of knowledge? Have you also wondered if they have the hours to get the job done on time? In summary, what influences a team's ability to reach goals?

Phillip: They are supposed to know. That is why they got hired.

Luis: Phillip, why are you here being coached by me?

Phillip: Because members of my team are unhappy with my style, and I need help.

Luis: So, you were hired to lead people effectively, yet they complain about your leadership. What does it say about your competence? And why should you get a free pass and they do not?

Phillip: Wow, it really does blow my mind how helpful this discussion has been. I have been so focused on others' failures and flaws that I have not paid attention to the log in my own eye! But, the truth is, yes, we are all being incompetent in some areas, myself included.

Luis: We all are, Phillip. We all have flaws and gaps. I propose setting a special session aside to learn management and supervisory tools and methods to help you diagnose performance. It seems that you are delegating without ensuring all the ducks are lined up. For instance, are you checking to see if your reports have the time and skills to deliver or the ability to coordinate amongst themselves to get things done?

Also, after results are in, or not, do you spend time with your team learning why things went well or not?

Phillip: For the most part, Luis, I have assumed they have what it takes to solve problems and meet goals. I do not follow up on results the way you are asking. I would welcome another learning session with you.

Luis: Deal! We will find time at the end of today's session.

Let's get back to our conversation on attributes and values (MTs).

Again, what were you attributing to the team when they missed the mark?

Phillip: That they were lazy or intentionally rebellious or difficult.

Luis: Now that you know about meaning intelligence and health, what new insights do you have about such attributions?

Phillip: If I understood the theory well, my judgments were not intelligent nor healthy. Now that I know that lack of time and skills (or other root causes) could be factored in the underperformance, I acknowledge I have not been helpful.

Luis: Is it fair to say you were judging rather than helping?

Phillip: Well, yes. That behavior explains why some of them were retreating (Attitude MT) and becoming frustrated with me.

Luis: Can you think about how your values influenced the attributions you made?

Phillip: As I said, I have high standards, but I learned I am not applying them intelligently.

Luis: The way I saw it, you had a clash of values. Why would I say that?

Phillip: Tell me, please.

Luis: You tell me how your high standards clash against the value MT of how people deserve to be treated. What you give priority to, and why.

Phillip: I understand. We covered this. My high standards on delivering work results contrast against my belief that people should be treated with respect.

Luis: Again, do they have to be incompatible?

Phillip: Not if I learn how to diagnose my team's performance and help instead of criticizing or judging.

Meaning Replacement and Realignment

Luis: And you will learn how to diagnose performance. What then will you do differently from this point forward?

Phillip: First, remember that being humane and respectful can be congruent with getting the right results. Second, I need to learn more about leadership and management, and third, follow a problem-solving approach rather than judge my team members.

Luis: What about remaining aware of what you are feeling, what it means, and where it can lead?

Phillip: Oh, yes, that too.

Luis: I propose that you may have a habituated response when angry or upset, Phillip. And generally, this habit needs to be dealt with intentionally. One cannot just wish it away. Or am I wrong thinking this might not be a problem for you?

Phillip: Yes, I still have this sense of despair when things are not going well. I do get anxious, and I can't always control myself. So I need to continue working on it. How can I go about it?

(Here is a great place to introduce the important step of replacing the flawed meanings that have led to the consequences the client has been experiencing. Up to this point, Phillip has been identifying what meanings have been leading to the actions he has displayed. Actions that have led to the problematic results he's looking to correct. To prevent his actions from yielding the negative impacts on

his employees, as well as on his interactions and relationships in his personal life, he must shift toward healthy and intelligent meanings. These new meanings will lead to more positive and uplifting actions and outcomes. By hearing that Phillip has decided and committed to improving, we can now proceed, hearing that there are no remaining resistances to changing and growing [blocks to meaning]. This is great progress!)

Luis: We need to plan a replacement approach from reactive to proactive in handling difficult situations. This approach would entail helping you strengthen your meanings, for instance, your values, and with the tools, I will teach you to solve differently. So we agreed to schedule a time today for a session on some management and quality tools I believe will help you. This skill-building includes learning alternate ways of communicating when in conflict.

Phillip: It makes sense to me, and I look forward to learning these methods.

Luis: Is your team still the target audience who will benefit from your improvement? As I mentioned in the early part of our first session, we need a pre and post-way to measure your progress and final success.

Phillip: Yes, my staff is still the target to measure.

Meaning Reintegration

Luis: Phillip, I propose that you share your improvement goals with your leader and team and ask them to help you as soon as possible. Would you be willing to do that?

Phillip: Why? I can understand my boss, but asking my reports for help in my development?

Luis: There is healing required here. Given what has happened, how much does your team trust you today?

Phillip: I see where you are going. But I will need your help. I have never done this before.

Luis: I am here to support you, Phillip. Of course, I will help you. The aim is to build or rebuild the trust of your team with you. Let us add to your learning how to design a team session to meet that goal. Would that work for you?

Philip: (Smiling) It will help me sleep better! I look forward to it.

Meaning Reinforcement and Sustainment

Luis: And I congratulate you for taking steps to improve yourself and to be true to your values, Phillip. I am confident that with your commitment to change, you will grow and improve and help others grow and improve as well.

Chapter Summary and Review

The AVR Method© helps people thrive in life. It has applications in therapy, coaching, counseling, consulting, and development. The goal of the method is to

- Identify and sustain meanings that add value to self and others
- Identify and replace harmful meanings with healthier options
- Help the client discover what gives meaning to life (i.e., meaning in life)
- Claim and assert one's meaning of life

The process finetunes the cooperation and agreement of the six types within the meaning-set. Increasing the content, quality, and harmony of the meaning type produces congruence. Robust and intelligent attributions, beliefs, and values will generate wholesome feelings and attitudes. As a result, we believe that groups, communities, organizations, and nations who share, promote, and practice meaningful ends will flourish.

The AVR Method© follows a sequence of seven phases:

1. Meaning Awareness
2. Meaning Analysis
3. Meaning Validation
4. Meaning Re-decision

5. Meaning Replacement and Realignment
6. Meaning Reintegration
7. Meaning Reinforcement and Sustainment

All responsible and ethical work between clients and practitioners should clarify goals, roles, processes, and norms upfront. In addition, it is helpful to have a standard contract for your private practice.

The method uses the *Logoteleology Identity Model in Action*. The practitioner can facilitate a developmental process through these two tools where the meaning discrepancy is reduced by increasing the meaning-set's content and quality and accuracy. Logoteleologists, or meaningful purpose psychology practitioners, are trained to master the developmental process responsibly and competently.

Reflection and Practice

1. Come up with an example of a situation where you would use the AVR Method© with a client. First, briefly explain how each of the seven steps would apply. Then, choose one step to omit and explain the impact on your client's improvement journey.
2. Why is role clarity a vital part of working with a client? What could the result of a lack of role clarity potentially be?

Chapter Eight

Conclusion

Summary and Next Steps

"True knowledge is knowledge of causes."
Francis Bacon

This book was written to explain and provide a practical, relevant application to meaningful purpose psychology's (MP) core elements. Our goal has been to benefit practitioners and others who will understand and apply MP methods through therapy and counseling, leadership, coaching, and other support services. In addition, individuals who seek to learn and apply MP on their own personal and interpersonal journeys will also benefit.

In the book's Introduction, we posed the three questions below. While reading this last summary and conclusion chapter we invite you to keep these questions in mind and reflect on them through the context of what you've learned.

Do my actions support what I want to happen in my life?
Do I know what the meaning of my life is and why that matters?
Am I personally connected to my life goals?

Chapter One: What is a Meaning?

The first chapter explained what meanings are and the crucial role they play in the quality of our lives. We learned that meaning (gr., Logos) is a singular aim backed by reasons, motives, and justifications. Moreover, meanings determine the behavioral agenda, and the actions spurred by such meanings produce consequences. Thus, if we are unhappy with the quality of our life and particular outcomes (e.g., consequences), we start by reviewing our meanings and ability to generate outcomes aligned with them. The good news is that by understanding meanings we, too, can determine, plan, and live a fulfilling existence.

We also learned that we could better understand ourselves and others and carry out specific meaning-improvement interventions through the construct of meaning. These six dynamic meaning types (i.e., meaning-construct) are Attributions, Beliefs, Values, Feelings, Attitudes, and Aims. Knowing their definition and role within the meaning-construct can help us grasp the specific "why" of our life and behavior and bring about targeted improvements to ensure meaning-set self-determination and harmony. As a model, the meaning-construct provides the framework to analyze our meanings. When analyzing a person's meaning (construct) content, we refer to it as their meaning-set.

We explained that meanings are either intelligent and healthy or unintelligent and unhealthy. An intelligent meaning is well-informed, empirical, and aligned with objective reality. Moreover, an intellectual meaning has a high quantity and quality of information. Hence, it is reliable and confident. On the other hand, an unintelligent meaning is ignorant and often relies on opinions, untested traditions, and hearsay or unfounded information. An unintelligent meaning is short on data to be based on, and what information it does have is low-quality. Therefore, our success in life depends on a consonant, reliable, truthful, proper, and dependable meaning-set. Consonant meaning-sets also deliver meaningful information, feelings, and aims.

A healthy meaning is loving, promotes peace and happiness, engages in activities that add value, and brings prosperity (i.e., is meaningful) to all stakeholders. In this way, the meaningful edifies, builds, is ethical, and brings the best out of oneself and others. On the other hand, dissonant, unhealthy, and flawed meanings harm the self and others.

There are two types of meaning-sets: Situational and Identity Meaning DNA Sets (IMDS). Situational meaning-sets (SMS) relate to behavior, and the IMDS relate to identity. A *Situational Meaning-set* is a momentary, narrative, sensory-filled, and affective collection of organized meaning types (MTs) primed and intended to respond to environmental demands. On the other hand, IMDS is a collection of organized meanings that highlight the uniqueness of a person's identity. The IMDS carries the psychological individuality and imprint of each human being. The IMDS determines our worldview. As a rule, Situational Meaning-sets will generate aims or intents consistent with the IMDS.

Why Meanings Matter

Meaning is what makes thinking and feeling possible. The best path for a happy and productive life is to ensure our meanings are both intelligent and healthy. Therefore, we encourage people to pursue a meaning of life that builds one's intellect and code of ethics to benefit all. Moreover, understanding that meanings have degrees of intelligence and health helps diagnose behavior and design and select meaningful solutions to improve the human condition. Meaning content analysis is made possible by understanding and leveraging the meaning-construct. It also allows the trained individual and practitioner to design and implement the appropriate improvements.

Chapter Two: What is Meaningful and Important?

Chapter two explains that humans yearn for love, peace and peace of mind, happiness, engagement in exciting and challenging activities, and prosperity. We call these the Five Meaningful Life Strivings. These meaningful states are a strong motivational force for all humans. However, our ability to achieve them depends on the quality of our meanings; how intelligent and healthy they are. Moreover, these yearnings follow a sequence, and there is synergy among them. For instance, if we wish to experience peace and peace of mind, we would be well-served to have positive and loving relationships with others.

All life problems, at any level, are the result of meanings and behavior that counter the Five Meaningful Life Strivings.

Three competencies support living up to the meaningful: Allow, Cooperate, and Transcend.

Why The Meaningful Matters

Logoteleology encourages people to give importance to what is meaningful and to reject and avoid the meaningless. Improvement can be achieved and sustained by remaining aware of our meanings and their quality (i.e., health and intelligence). Conversely, we can ignore what is meaningful at our peril. Both experience and empirical findings demonstrate that the meaningless is the cause of unhappiness and hardship. We believe that the meaningful path creates the best conditions to thrive in life.

Chapter three: The Identity Formula

In Chapter Three, we answered the question, "Who am I?" Identity is what makes us uniquely recognizable to ourselves and others. We leveraged sociologists Peter J. Burke and Jan E. Stets' *Identity Theory* to explain three identity meanings:

1. person identity, or what makes an individual distinct from others
2. social identity, or our membership in groups, either default, obligatory, or self-selected.
3. role identity, or the role we play as a member of a group

Identities have two components, physical (body) and psychological (mind). Moreover, identities are formed by antecedents, such as our biological DNA, family influence, culture, accumulated learning, life experiences, and current situation and context. Identity theory can help us understand the meaning of our life. It does so by pointing to our uniqueness and calling, to meet the needs of others through roles. We can determine our sense of self by defining and employing our talents and potential to benefit those we interact with (social groups) through specific roles (e.g., spouse, parent, leader, team member).

We introduced the Logoteleology Identity Model (LIM) composed of meaning, motivation, and purpose to explain

- the cognitive and sensory elements of meanings
- how meanings determine intensity and type of motivation
- how motivation or energy-in-motion fuels purposeful action through skills

The LIM establishes the framework to plan, write, and assert a meaningful life purpose. As in, "I am a weather forecaster (identity) who deeply enjoys (motivation) reporting weather conditions (purpose) to help people plan their lives (meaning)." LIM's expanded version, LIMA or Logoteleology Identity Model in Action, is designed, among other things, to help the individual understand why consequences match or fulfill the intended meaning. Guided by a competent practitioner, the goal is to help the client increase meaningful meaning accuracy to reduce or eliminate meaningless outcomes.

Why do Identities Matter?

Logoteleology uses practical and relevant methods to help uncover and understand a person's current default meaning of life. In addition, it can aid in developing and successfully implementing a *meaningful* meaning of life for individuals. Therefore, the Logoteleology Identity Model can be an essential tool to help take charge, control, and self-determine a person's life calling. Understanding identity also allows us to ensure person, social, and role alignment. Such knowledge reminds us to remain faithful and to steer our lives first and foremost through our person identities. In these identities lies the true essence and meaning potential of an individual's life. Hence, knowing and leveraging the LIM help us to effectively and efficiently self-regulate our meanings and behaviors to meaningful ends.

Chapter Four: Motivation

Our ability to accomplish life's meanings and their tasks depend on the quality of our commitment. Therefore, motivation (gr. Thelos) is a component of the Logoteleology Identity Model (LIM). The moment a meaning becomes a determining motive is known as *telosponse*. Meanings provoke telosponses. As energy-in-motion or directed energy, motivation's role is to fuel purposeful behavior. The chapter explains that motivation has two elements; energy and direction. In other words, motivation offers a degree of power and a path or course. Therefore, the meaning type attitude plays a significant role in determining the strength and direction of the motivational force.

We learned that the construct of motivation's direction has four elements:

- Will (intrinsic): willingly motivated by curiosity and intellectual honesty; "I want to" disposition
- Drive (extrinsic): a compulsive, uncontrollable response or urge; "I have to" disposition
- Demotivation (extrinsic/intrinsic): avoidance or unwillingness to socially engage with others or carry out an activity. Demotivation can occur because of a sense of helplessness, apathy, rebelliousness or defiance, or distrust; "I don't want to" disposition
- Tactical Retreat (intrinsic): a diplomatic and courageous disengagement from a toxic or potentially unpleasant situation or outcome; "I choose not to" disposition

The quality of a motivational force depends on a Meaningful Meaning Ecology of three meaningful variables:

- Goals: aspirational ends for good
- Processes: clear, relevant, and enabling purposes, roles, methods and procedures, guidelines, and tools
- Settings: edifying and allowing environment and culture

Why does Motivation Matter?

By understanding motivation and the meaning-construct, we can consciously or deliberately assess its energy level and direction and determine its meaning. Moreover, we can quickly determine if the root cause lies in the LIM's meaning or purpose components and solve the problem with great precision.

Chapter Five: Blocks to Meaning

This chapter describes how a person's worldview is a double-edged sword. On the one hand, a worldview gives us a sense of predictability through shared and familiar or common meanings (e.g., culture, language, surroundings, traditions). Yet, on the other hand, different worldviews and their meanings can either generate curiosity leading to learning or have a distracting, avoiding, and even destructive effect. A dominant and obstinate worldview leads to selective thinking and filtering of inconvenient and uncomfortable information, even when it is empirically valid and meaningful to consider and follow. This phenomenon explains why problems persist and remain unresolved. Hence, meaningful purpose psychology aims to promote discerning and pursuing unbiased truth and reality through intelligent and healthy meanings.

Calcified meanings prevent us from considering all relevant information. As a result, calcification can and does generate unintelligent and even unhealthy meanings. Meaning-calcification *provokes meaning-sclerosis* or the absence of critical information for sound judgment, success, and thriving. Hence, people can live their daily life as if it is grounded in unbiased truth and reality. However, the cost of living this way can vary, and its effect can be experienced in the short or the long term, but an ultimate price will be paid. The MP method provides a path to understand the quality of our meanings, remove irrelevant and false information from our mental data bank, and replace it with intelligent, healthy, and reality-based alternatives.

Why do Blocks to Meaning Matter?

Understanding and countering meaning-calcification and meaning-sclerosis can be liberating and propel us forward with energy to fulfill what life calls upon us to do. A life free of pretensions (e.g., imposter syndrome) and false beliefs, values, and attributions will better allow us to understand and respond to the demands and opportunities as they arise. Blocks to meaning affect all areas of our lives, and removing such obstacles and replacing them with truth and integrity will have us experience freedom as we never imagined possible.

Chapter Six: Meaning of Life and Meaning in Life

The meaning of life is intimately tied to identity. Meaning of life is the active fulfillment of a personal mission. It answers the question, "Why do I live?" A meaningful life can be self-determined or run its course scripted by the past, in default mode without understanding how it influences our choices. The different roles we occupy in life (e.g., parent, leader, student, professional) within our group identities (e.g., family, employment, nationality) should have a meaningful purpose to accomplish. Moreover, these meaningful collective purposes should be submitted to and aligned with our identities' meaning of life. In other words, we should strive to fulfill the personal meaning of our life through the roles we occupy within our membership in groups.

To achieve *meaning in life* is to live a meaningful life. A meaning in life describes what the individual finds motivating and gratifying and aligned with their natural strengths and preferences. The Five Meaningful Life Strivings of love, peace/peace of mind, happiness, interest/engagement, and eventual prosperity (i.e., the meaningful) give life meaning or fulfill the definition of meaning in life. Thus, knowing what brings meaning in life is to know what gives meaning to life.

MP methods encourage people to discover the meaning of their lives and fulfill it through those life-enhancing sources that fill us with love, peace, joy, fascination, and prosperity.

Why does knowing What is Meaning of Life and Meaning in Life Matter?

If consequences are the outcomes of our meanings, we are well-served to study our default or self-determined meaning of life and assess how aligned this is with what gives our life meaning (i.e., meaning in life). Appreciating the difference can also help us answer fundamental questions about the human condition, such as suffering and despair and thriving and success. This knowledge can also place us in the driver's seat to determine who we will be and how we will live, for whom, and to what meaningful benefit.

Chapter Seven: The AVR Method©

This chapter describes MP's prime seven-step process from meaning awareness to reintegration and sustainment. The seven-step process includes meaning awareness, analysis, validation, re-decision, replacement and realignment, integration, and reinforcement and sustainment. It has broad applications benefiting coaching, therapy, counseling, and consulting practitioners and their clients. In a nutshell, the AVR Method© ultimately helps clients live a meaningful life by increasing meaning intelligence, health, and accuracy. The client explores the content and quality of their meanings and determines what improvements and alignments are required to fulfill their meaning of life in a meaningful way.

The method leverages other MP models (e.g., meaning-construct, LIM, LIMA) to increase awareness, understand the meaning, and bring about intelligent, healthy, and accurate improvements. The goal is not just to solve a particular challenge but also to increase the ability to perceive better and select meaningful responses.

Why does knowing the AVR Method© Matter?

Anyone who has a good understanding of the process can follow the steps to meet their goals. Moreover, those interested in building proficiency in the methodology can pursue certification to develop the abilities and confidence to help others. The process is intuitive, logical, and practical. It can help the practitioner plan the approach, follow that plan, know where things stand, and determine the next steps.

Action Steps

We started this chapter quoting Francis Bacon: "True knowledge is knowledge of causes." Aligned with Bacon's quote, we defined meaning as a singular aim backed by reasons, motives, and justifications. And since reasons, motives, and justifications are causes, meaningful purpose psychology studies and remedies or enhances the "why" (causes) of situations to improve the human condition.

As we claimed in the Introduction, we wrote this book for us—as individuals and communities—to live a worthwhile life that benefits all, without exceptions. We should all embrace and practice what is meaningful and create those conditions where humanity can thrive.

In this book's introduction, we used an analogy of the milestones in life and the steps in between them. Is it much easier to recognize and connect to the meaningful experiences of milestones, but it is in the steps between these milestones where most of life is lived. Our purpose throughout this text has been to introduce you, the reader, to the ways that logoteleology is used to do just that, to identify and connect to the meaning that each of us has, and through that meaningful living to thrive and help others thrive as well.

Thank you for reading and sharing this meaningful purpose with us.

Acknowledgments

"When we give cheerfully and accept gratefully, everyone is blessed."
~ Maya Angelou ~

We are filled with gratitude to Nahir Rivera, Christian Marrero, Isabel Persuitte, and Christopher L. Marrero for their insights and feedback to improve this book's content (and grammar). We appreciate so much each of them taking the time to review the manuscript and provide feedback and suggestions.

We thank Khalil Rivera for his invaluable support, guidance, and insight on design elements that would aid us in our choosing a cover for this book. Khalil did a masterful design with Luis' first book, The Path to a Meaningful Purpose: *Psychological Foundations of Logoteleology.* We are fortunate to gain from his wisdom and experience.

We, too, appreciate the work of graphic designer Matthew Hernandez, who improved our primitive versions of our artwork.

We also thank Mary Ann Kasperson for her willingness to read through the manuscript and the benefit of providing her suggestions.

We thank our spouses, Nahir Rivera and Nahir Marrero, for their patience and support as we borrowed so many hours of family time to spend on this work to benefit others.

We are also thankful for the invaluable learning we gained while practicing meaningful purpose psychology with clients, friends, and colleagues. You have each assisted in supporting our purpose of helping others live a meaningful life.

About the Boston Institute
for Meaningful Purpose

Our Mantra: *To enable people and institutions to succeed in their meaningful purpose.*

The Boston Institute for Meaningful Purpose is the hub of meaningful purpose psychology, logoteleology, research and development, and Second Wave Organization Development or OD 2.0.

The Institute was founded by Luis A. Marrero, M.A., RODP, MLP, in 1986 in Boston, Massachusetts. Daniel E. Persuitte, B.A., MLP, joined the institute in 2017 and is a managing partner.

Through this partnership Luis and Dan lead the institute forward by growing and refining the theories and methods of meaningful purpose psychology and creating new content and ways to share it. This centralization point serves as a platform from which Luis and Dan collaborate on furthering the purpose of MP to enable people and institutions to thrive and succeed.

The Boston Institute for Meaningful Purpose currently has its main office in Westfield, Massachusetts, with a field office in Deltona, Florida from which it serves individuals, groups, and global companies in various countries.

The Boston Institute for Meaningful Purpose
11 Belmont Street
Westfield, MA 01085

www.bostonimp.com

Glossary

A

ACT: The three elements (Allow, Cooperate, Transcend) of interaction with the external environment in support of a meaningful state. These three elements are competencies that help fulfill the Five Meaningful Life Strivings. Without *ACT,* the pursuit of the five strivings is met with environmental discord that can easily impede the ability to achieve true meaningfulness.

Activity Trap: An expression coined by Peter Drucker. The risk of becoming so busy with activity so as to forget and miss the aim of that activity.

Anádras*i*sponse: Related to feedback. The motivation flow step where the consequence is channeled and received for decoding to determine if there is a match between meaning intent and consequence.

Apathy: a willing and sincere lack of interest in a subject, thing, situation, or person. Logoteleologists assist the indifferent individual in determining and committing to a meaningful and intrinsically motivating life task dedicated to benefiting oneself and others.

Apórroiasponse: Related to aftereffect. Motivation flow step that consists of an impact with a consequence then leads to anadrasisponse.

Aspirational Striving: An element of the Aim meaning type related to motivation indicating being compelled toward a goal, a need, or desire.

Available Power: (see Energy)

AVR Method© Phases: The seven steps, or stages, to the AVR Method© (Meaning Awareness, Analysis, Validation, Re-decision, Replacement, Reintegration, and Reinforcement).

B

C

Cognitive Dissonance: Mental discord resulting from a disconnect between meaning types and behavior, attitudes, and actions.

Compulsory Drive: An element of the Aim meaning type related to motivation indicating an extrinsic push toward something, as in being compelled or coerced.

Congruent Narrative: Within a meaning-set, meaning type content that aligns to the task or challenge.

Consequence: An element of the Logoteleology Identity Model in Action that reveals the contact's response and that response's effect.

Consonant meaning-set: Meaning-sets that render meaningful information, feelings, and aims.

Contact: An element of the Logoteleology Identity Model in Action that is the target of our attention and the overall context and setting.

D

Default Meaning of Life: A person's meaning of life can be default—that is, driven by identities that the individual may be unaware of either partially or in full.

Direction: Also referred to as steered energy, the role of direction is to channel or guide energy in a way that is determined by meanings. Direction can be willed, driven, demotivated, and a tactical retreat (See Motivation Types).

Dissonant meaning-set: Meaning-sets that have faulty or meaningless content, creating discord.

Distrustful: People become distrustful when they sense they cannot rely on others or conditions, leading to distancing or moving away, at least until trust is restored.

Drásisponse: Related to Action. A motivation step where exists a spur to respond, leading to aporroiasponse.

E

Energy/Motivational Intensity: Available power can vary in intensity ranging from non-existent to very high.

Extrinsic: Originating from outside the self; External.

F

Feedback: In the Meaningful Purpose Identity Model, it helps the individual determine if their meanings were fulfilled.

G

Group Meaning Alignment: A state of alignment and harmony amongst members of a group. Misalignment of meanings leads to discord, lack of role clarity, and causes rifts between group members.

H

I

Identity Meaning DNA Set (IMDS): a collection of organized meanings that highlight the uniqueness of a person's identity. As in a meaning of life, the IMDS can be default if not self-determined.

Incongruent Narrative: Meaning type content within a meaning-set that is misaligned to a task or challenge.

Intended-Outcome Model: A model used by Logoteleologists to diagnose and improve option selection. The model places consequence into one of four quadrants base on scales of *intention* and *outcome*.

Interpersonal Meaning Accuracy: Accuracy of meaning measurement related to others.

Intrapersonal Congruent Meaning-set: Harmonious narratives where all six meaning types within a meaning-set are in sync to meet the challenge, increasing the odds of meaning accuracy.

Intrapersonal Incongruent Meaning-set: Competing meaning-set content where narratives are misaligned to a challenge's needs.

Intrapersonal Meaning Accuracy: Accuracy of meaning measurement related to the self.

Intrinsic: Originating from the self; Internal.

J

K

L

Lasting (formal) Groups: People connected through a commitment to fulfill a common task that requires investment in resources, such as time and diligent effort.

Like/Don't Like Continuum: An attitudinal scale ranging from don't like to like referring to the meanings that drive direction. This scale determines motivation's intensity and direction of energy.

LIM Formula: Identity = Meaning + Motivation + Purpose (I=Me+Mo+P). See also Logoteleology Identity Model.

LIMA Formula: Identity = Meaning + Motivation + Purpose + Contact + Consequence. (I=Me+Mo+P+Co=C) (See also Logoteleology Identity Model in Action.)

Logoteleologist: A certified practitioner of meaningful purpose psychology. Logoteleologists carry out meaning, motivation, and purpose analysis to help people determine and live a meaningful life. The process includes helping the clients to understand their motives and intentions to discover what makes a meaning healthy and follow an edifying process for human thriving through self-determined ways.

Logoteleology: (meaningful purpose psychology) The study of the meanings that allow individuals and communities to thrive. An optimistic and positive science describes how people and organizations give meaning to the self, others, and situations; and how such meanings can and do lead to a consequence. Logoteleology seeks to increase meaningful meaning accuracy from intent to consequence.

Logoteleology Identity Model (LIM): A formula illustrating the formation of identities through meaning, purpose, and motivation or Identity = Meaning + Motivation + Purpose (I=Me+Mo+P).

Logoteleology Identity Model in Action (LIMA): The addition of Contact and Consequence to the LIM (see Logoteleology Identity Model) in order to study interpersonal transactions, impact, and consequences, where Identity = Meaning + Motivation + Purpose + Contact + Consequence (I=Me+Mo+P+Co=C).

Logoteleology Motivation Formula (Mo=E+D): A logoteleological formula where Motivation = Energy + Direction.

Logotherapy: A form of meaning-based psychology developed by Viktor Frankl that posits humankind is motivated by a "will to meaning."

M

Meaning: A singular intent or goal back by reasons, motives, and justifications. Something meant or intended; In communication, an idea expressed by using words, symbols, etc.

Meaning Antecedent: Five factors that precede and influence meaning-constructs. The five meaning antecedents are Biogenetic DNA, Psychosocial Influence, Culture, Accumulated Learning, and Current situation and context.

Meaning-calcification: The inability, refusal, or antipathy to perceive and respond to sensible incoming data.

Meaning Congruence: A state of alignment obtained when all meaning types agree, cooperate, and follow through.

Meaning-construct: The *meaning-construct* is a theoretical model containing, defining, and explaining the dynamics of six meaning types (Attributes, Beliefs, Values, Feelings, Attitudes, Aims). The individual and unique meanings that apply to the meaning types. (see also: Meaning Type).

Meaning DNA (see Psychological Meaning DNA): The content and essence of personality or identity shaped by the individual's meaning-set.

Meaning Exchange: A conveyance of meanings between two or more parties; Communication.

Meaning Exchange Economies: The exchange of meanings to meet goals. Interpersonal interactions to satisfy the needs, wants, and goals of stimulation, recognition, and care.

Meaning/Important Quadrant: Used to determine the level of importance corresponding with the meaningful and meaningless. The four elements of the quadrant are Meaningful, Important, Meaningless, and Unimportant. Meaningful does not necessarily equal importance since one can place importance on the meaningless (though they should not).

Meaning in life: Describes what an individual finds to be motivating and gratifying; what makes life worth living.

Meaning of life: The active fulfillment of one's mission, predicated upon meanings unique to each individual. Absent conscious awareness, a person's meaning of life can be default—that is, driven by identities that the individual may be unaware of either partially or in full. (see Default Meaning of Life and Self-determined Meaning of Life).

Meaning-sclerosis: The absence of critical information for sound judgment, success, and thriving. Meaning-sclerosis is the outcome of meaning-calcification.

Meaning-set: Composed of six meaning types: Attributes, Beliefs, Values, Feelings, Attitudes, Aims. The content and interaction of meaning types serve as a processing mechanism in human behavior, taking in information and determining how to respond, adapt, and thrive in an environment. The meaning-set is critical in determining the category and level of motivation and purposeful action.

Meaning-set Analysis: A process used by Logoteleologists to diagnose and improve individual, group, organizational, national, and international meanings.

Meaning Task: Meanings are called upon to perform two complementary tasks, to Intend or to set a goal to Justify (Reason).

Meaning type: six factors or types (Beliefs, Values, Attitudes, Attributes, Feelings, Aims) related to reasons, motives, justifications, intentions, and goals. Meaning Types are the components of a meaning.

Meaningful Meaning Ecology: A meaningful-motivational environment consisting of the three elements Goals, Processes, Settings.

Meaningful Meaning Exchange: A valid, honest, and transparent conveyance of meanings.

Meaningful Purpose Psychology: Also commonly abbreviated to MP (see Logoteleology).

Meaningful Purpose Psychology Practitioner: (see Logoteleologist)

Meaningless Meaning Exchange: A deceptive or vailed conveyance of meanings.

Motivation Types: The four paths of energy (Will, Drive, Demotivate, Tactical Retreat) can flow determined by the underlying meanings.

N

Natural Attributes: Likings, inclinations, talents, and strengths inherent in every human being.

O

P

Person Identity: Based on the work of sociologists Peter j. Burke and Jan E. Stets, an identity formed in early life by our DNA, our family, culture, life experiences, expectations we place on ourselves, and continuous learning and improvement.

Preventative Methods: Actions focused on content and quality of person, social, and role identities to ensure healthy Person, Social, and Role Identities (PSRI) meaning-sets.

PSRI: An acronym referring to the three types of identities (Person, Social, and Role Identities).

Psychological Meaning DNA: A collection of organized meanings possessed by each individual that includes a definition of who they are, a justification for why they live, and any life goals or missions. It carries the psychological individuality and imprint of each human being.

Purpose: Actions or activities that fulfill meanings; the carrying-out of a meaning. Purpose is the application of skills and competencies.

Q

R

Rebellious: an attitude fed by fear and anger. Energy is channeled to push against (resist) or to separate (move away).

Remedial Support: a specialized support service for each identity type required when preventive methods are not followed.

Role Identity: Based on the work of sociologists Peter j. Burke and Jan E. Stets, an identity where there exist duties to fulfill, requirements of abilities and personal traits to do well, and a need to interact with other group members (e.g., interdependence) to achieve the assumed common task.

S

Self-determined Meaning of Life: An individual follows convictions and behavior unaffected by extrinsic (external) forces. Hence, a self-determined meaning of life entails freely choosing one's identity and life mission.

Situational Meaning-set (SMS): a momentary, narrative, sensory-filled, and affective collection of organized meaning types primed and intended to respond to environmental demands.

Social (Group) Identity: Based on the work of sociologists Peter j. Burke and Jan E. Stets, an identity as part of a group or organization that provides members a sense of solidarity through shared interests, experiences, values, beliefs, and feelings. Group identity can be default, obligatory, or voluntary.

Steered Energy: (see Direction)

T

Telosponse: Related to Purpose. An action in the steps of the motivation flow that determines energy and direction, becoming a thelosponse.

Temporary (informal) Groups: People connected through a commonality, coming about through casual and short-lived interactions.

The AVR Method©: A foundational logoteleological procedure designed to help individuals, groups, organizations, and even nations to examine and (when required) improve their meanings.

The Client-Practitioner Contract: An agreement between a client and practitioner meant to ensure responsible and ethical work that lays out goals, roles, processes, and norms upfront.

The Five Meaningful Life Strivings: Also referred to as The Meaningful Path, the five elements (Love, Peace and peace of mind, Happiness, Engagement, and Prosperity) of a meaningful state or experience. These are five meaningful states that humans yearn for and strive to experience in life.

The Helpless: A person experiences helplessness when they lack the influence or competence to carry out essential tasks. A goal of MP is to help individuals with helpless symptoms to gain internal confidence, competence, and other resources to achieve meaningful goals. When conditions cannot be changed, the helpless are encouraged to find meaning in the experience rather than feeling victimized by circumstances.

The Meaningful Path: (see The Five Meaningful Life Strivings)

Thelosponse: Related to Will. Motivation flow step that consists of a volley of impulses that fuel a response leading to drasisponse.

Transactional Meaning: Meanings exchanged within the meaning-set (internal) and the external environment to meet the daily needs and wants in life and satisfy innate aspirations to improve and thrive.

Transformational Meaning: Can be self-oriented or other-oriented. Self-oriented transformational meanings seek the person to grow and be validated by others, while other-oriented transformational meanings support *others'* desire to improve.

Type-A Personality: A temperament characterized by excessive drive and competitiveness, hostility, an unrealistic sense of time urgency, inappropriate ambition, a reluctance to provide self-evaluation, a tendency to emphasize quantity of output over quality, and a need for control. [97]

Index

f denotes figure; *t* denotes table

A

accuracy
    achieving meaning accuracy, 122
    defined, 122, 129
    interpersonal accuracy, 124
    interpersonal meaning accuracy,
        123–124, 170
    intrapersonal accuracy, 124
    intrapersonal meaning accuracy,
        122–123, 170
    meaningless meaning accuracy,
        122, 129
ACT (allow cooperate, transcend), xxii,
    44, 60, 83, 122, 167
activity trap, 77, 78, 167
Adler, Alfred, 8, 13, 96, 97, 98, 101
aim-goal, 18
aim-intent, 18
aims
    aim-goal, 18
    aim-intent, 18
    congruent narratives and
        incongruent narratives of,
        125*t*
    examples of healthy and unhealthy
        ones, 26*t*

    intelligent and unintelligent
        descriptions and examples
        of, 29*t*
    as meaning type, xxii, 16–18
    practitioner questions and
        statements about, 136
    role of, 24
    sample questions to increase
        awareness of, 100
    types of, 18–19
Ajzen, Icek, 73
allow, as A in ACT, xxii, 44, 50, 60, 83,
    90, 122, 156
anádrasisponse, 86, 87*f*, 167
Ansbacher, Heinz L., 110
Ansbacher, Rowena R., 110
apathy
    defined, 167
    as one of four possible reasons for
        demotivation, 75, 80–81
apórroiasponse, 86, 87*f*, 167
aspirational striving, 16, 167
attentional allocation, 95
attitudes
    congruent narratives and
        incongruent narratives of,
        125*t*
    examples of healthy and unhealthy
        ones, 26*t*

intelligent and unintelligent
descriptions and examples
of, 29t
as meaning type, xxii, 16
practitioner questions and
statements about, 136
role of, 24
sample questions to increase
awareness of, 100
attributes
congruent narratives and
incongruent narratives of,
125t
examples of healthy and unhealthy
ones, 25t
intelligent and unintelligent
descriptions and examples
of, 27t
as meaning type, xxii, 12–13
natural attributes, 116–117, 174
practitioner questions and
statements about, 135
role of, 23
sample questions to increase
awareness of, 99–100
attribution error, 95
AVR Method©
benefits of, 130
client-practitioner contract,
130–131
defined, 120, 127, 176
goal of, 121, 127
and LIMA, 132–134, 132f
and meaning-construct, 134–135
phases/stages of, xxvi, 126–
128, 168
Phillip's case study, 137–151
as proprietary MP framework
for meaning analysis and
improvement, xxi

use of by certified logoteleologists,
128–129
as usually complemented by LIM,
127, 128

B

Bacon, Francis, 162, 153
Baumeister, Roy, 15
Beckhard, Richard, 31
beliefs
congruent narratives and
incongruent narratives of,
125t
examples of healthy and unhealthy
ones, 25t
intelligent and unintelligent
descriptions and examples
of, 28t
as meaning type, xxii, 13–14
practitioner questions and
statements about, 135
role of, 24
sample questions to increase
awareness of, 100
as source of knowledge, 13
biases, 14, 21, 94, 95, 97, 98, 121
blind spots, 40, 95, 96, 121
blocks, to meaning awareness, 93,
95, 121
Boston Institute for Meaningful
Purpose, 165
Burke, Peter J., 53, 104, 107
Burns, James MacGregor, 43

C

client-practitioner contract, 130–
131, 177
cognitive dissonance, 93, 168
commitment, escalation to, 95
compatibility, defined, 123, 129

competencies, 69, 83, 88, 90, 106, 117.
    See also ACT (allow cooperate,
    transcend)
compulsory drive, 16, 168
confirmation bias, 95
congruence
    defined, 124
    meaning congruence, 124, 172
congruent narrative, 125, 125*f*, 168
consequence
    defined, 168
    as one of six components of LIMA,
        65, 66
    practitioner questions about, 134
    types of, 66*f*
consonant meaning-sets, 22, 24, 168
contact
    as one of six components of LIMA,
        64, 65, 168
    practitioner questions about, 133
cooperate, as C in ACT, xxii, 44, 50,
    60, 83, 90, 122, 156
cooperation, defined, 5
coping mechanisms, 95
Csikszentmihalyi, Mihaly, 84, 113

D

Deci, Edward L., 113
default meaning of life, xxvi, 8, 35, 107,
    108–110, 114, 168
default social identity, 54, 59*t*
demotivate
    as one of four paths of energy,
        74, 79
    as type of motivation, 77*f*
demotivation, four possible reasons
    for, 75
direction
    as component of motivation,
        74, 74*f*
    defined, 74, 169

disingenuous apathy, 80–81
dissonant meaning-sets, 22, 24, 169
distrustful
    defined, 169
    as one of four possible reasons for
        demotivation, 75, 82
drásisponse, 86, 87*f*, 169
drive
    as one of four paths of energy, 74,
        76–79
    as type of motivation, 77*f*
Drucker, Peter, 167
Dweck, Carol S., 14, 34

E

ego-defense mechanisms, 95
Einstein, Albert, 92
energy
    as component of motivation, 74
    defined, 74, 75, 169
    four paths of, 74, 75, 174
    steered energy, 74, 75, 176
Energy/Motivational Intensity, 73*f*
engagement/interest
    as Meaningful Life Striving, xxii,
        60, 116
    as one of five conditions of
        meaningful state/
        experience, 43, 83, 122
Epictetus, 120
escalation to commitment, 95
external transacting meanings, 21, 22
extrinsic, defined, 169

F

Fabry, Joseph B., 11, 14–15, 16
feedback
    defined, 169
    as one of six components of LIMA,
        65, 66–67
    practitioner questions about, 134

feelings
  congruent narratives and
    incongruent narratives of,
    125*t*
  examples of healthy and unhealthy
    ones, 26*t*
  intelligent and unintelligent
    descriptions and examples
    of, 28*t*
  as meaning type, xxii, 15–16
  practitioner questions and
    statements about, 136
  role of, 24
  sample questions to increase
    awareness of, 100
Five Meaningful Life Strivings/Five
  Strivings, xxii, 43, 48, 60, 83,
  116, 122, 177
flow, according to
  Csikszentmihalyi, 113
formal groups, 56, 57, 171
Frankl, Viktor, 2, 5, 15, 19, 35, 71,
  76, 172
Frederickson, Barbara L., 3, 19, 86, 99

G

genuine apathy, 80
Gibb, Jack, 31
GI-GO (Garbage In—Garbage
  Out), 96
glossary, 167–177
group meaning alignment, 31, 169
group meaning misalignment, 31

H

happiness
  as Meaningful Life Striving, xxii,
    60, 83, 116, 122
  as one of five conditions of
    meaningful state/
    experience, 43

helpless, as one of four possible
  reasons for demotivation, 75,
  79–80, 177

I

identity
  components of, 55, 60, 64
  default social identity, 54, 59*t*
  defined, 52, 55
  as expressed as noun, 61
  formation of, 59–60
  obligatory social identity, 54,
    55, 59*t*
  person, social, and role identities
    (PSRI), 58
  person identity, 53, 104, 105–106,
    107, 175
  role identity, 57–58, 104–105,
    107, 176
  role of, 55
  social (group) identity, 54–57, 104,
    107, 176
  types of, 53–59, 59*t*, 104, 107
  voluntary social identity, 59*t*
  why they matter, 68
Identity Meaning DNA Set (IMDS),
  xxii, 9, 31, 33–34, 35–36, 170
Identity Theory (Burke and Stets), 53
IKAGAI model, 43
Ikes, William, 124
important, as contrasted with
  unimportant, 47, 47*f*, 48, 49
impostor syndrome, 95
inclinations, defined, 116–117
incongruence, reducing of, 126
incongruent meaning-sets, examples
  of, 125
incongruent narrative, 125, 125*f*,
  126, 170
informal groups, 56–57, 176
Intended-Outcome Model, 66, 66*f*, 170

interest/engagement
    as Meaningful Life Striving, xxii,
        60, 116
    as one of five conditions of
        meaningful state/
        experience, 43, 83, 122
internal transacting meanings, 21, 22
interpersonal accuracy, 124
interpersonal meaning accuracy, 123–
    124, 170
intrapersonal accuracy, 124
intrapersonal congruent meaning-sets,
    125, 170
intrapersonal meaning accuracy, 122–
    123, 170
intrinsic, defined, 170

J

Jefferson, Thomas, 45
justification, xx, 2, 3, 4, 5, 7, 10, 11, 18,
    38, 39, 61, 93, 154, 162

K

knowledge, as source of belief, 13

L

lasting groups, 56, 57, 171
Legrand, Dorothée, 61
life-goals, as way to define default
    meaning of life, 109
like/don't like continuum, 16, 56, 73,
    75, 171
likings, defined, 116
logoteleologist, defined, 171
logoteleology, defined, 171
Logoteleology Identity Model in Action
    (LIMA)
    AVR Method© and, 132–134, 132f
    components of, 65
    defined, 85, 86
    described, 63–64

diagnosing through, 67f
formula for, 171, 172
graphic of, xxiv, 63f, 87f
use of, xxiv
Logoteleology Identity Model (LIM)
    defined, xxiii
    described, 60–63
    diagnosing through, 67
    formula for, 171, 172
    graphic of, xxiii, 61f
    purpose of, xxiv
    as usually complementing AVR
        Method©, 127, 128
Logoteleology Motivation Formula,
    73f, 172
logotherapy
    according to Frankl, 15
    defined, 172
love
    as Meaningful Life Striving, xxii,
        60, 83, 116, 122
    as one of five conditions of
        meaningful state/
        experience, 43

M

Márquez, Gabriel García, 101
Marrero, Luis A., xxi, 137
meaning
    accessing of, 121–122
    according to Frankl, 2
    according to Frederickson, 3
    blocks to meaning awareness, 93,
        95, 121
    composition of, 11
    defined, 2–4, 172
    as determining worldview, 93, 121
    faulty meanings, 97
    as having consequences, 7
    meaningless meanings, 97

as one of six components of
LIMA, 65
as one of three components of
identity, 55, 60, 61f, 64
practitioner questions about, 132
as psychological DNA, 7
relevance of, 10–11
role of, 61
as setting the agenda and
guaranteeing and
explaining the outcome, 1
tasks performed by, 4, 11
transactional meaning, 177
transformational meaning, 177
meaning accuracy
achievement of, 122
interpersonal meaning accuracy,
123–124, 170
intrapersonal meaning accuracy,
122–123, 170
meaningless meaning accuracy,
122, 129
meaning analysis
in Phillip's case study, 141–143
as stage/phase of AVR Method©,
126, 127
meaning antecedents
defined, 172
as forming worldview, 94
list of, 35, 55, 59–60, 93
as way to define default meaning
of life, 109
meaning awareness
in Phillip's case study, 138–141
as stage/phase of AVR Method©,
126, 127
meaning congruence
achieving of, 124
defined, 172
meaning currency, 23
meaning discrepancy

reducing of, 122, 126, 127, 152
strengthening of, 124
meaning DNA, 4, 7, 9, 36, 59, 60, 93,
94, 173
meaning exchange, 3, 5, 21, 22, 24, 173
meaning exchange economies, 23–
24, 173
meaning imprint, 35, 59
meaning in life
as answering questions, 115
as complex, xxvi
congruent meaning of life and
meaning in life, 115
defined, 113, 173
as not always benign, 114, 115
role of, 115
meaning of life
concept of, 103
congruent meaning of life and
meaning in life, 115
default meaning of life, xxvi, 8, 35,
107, 108–110, 114, 168
defined, 108, 113, 173
elements in meaningful one, 112
MP's framework for, 103–106
self-determined meaning of life,
xxvi, 35, 107, 111, 176
standards for analyzing, validating,
modifying, and improving
of, 116
types of, 108
meaning re-decision
in Phillip's case study, 144–145
as stage/phase of AVR Method©,
126, 127
meaning reinforcement or sustainment
in Phillip's case study, 151
as stage/phase of AVR
Method©, 128
meaning reintegration
in Phillip's case study, 150–151

as stage/phase of AVR
Method©, 128
meaning replacement and realignment
in Phillip's case study, 149–150
as stage/phase of AVR
Method©, 128
meaning task, 174
meaning type intensity profiles, 33*t*
meaning types (MTs)
analysis of, 9
defined, 174
graphic of, 12*f*
healthy and unhealthy ones,
25–26*t*
list of, xxii, 10, 12–18, 23–24
use of term, 11
meaning validation
in Phillip's case study, 143–144
as stage/phase of AVR Method©,
126, 127
meaning-calcification, 94, 95–98, 172
meaning-construct, 11–12, 20, 36–38,
134–136, 172
meaningful, as contrasted with
meaningless, 45–46, 48
meaningful ecology, components of,
75. *See also* meaningful meaning
ecology
meaningful goals
defined, 83
as element of meaningful meaning
ecology, 83*f*
meaningful meaning ecology, 83–84,
83*f*, 174
meaningful meaning exchange, 174
meaningful processes
defined, 83
as element of meaningful meaning
ecology, 83*f*
meaningful purpose psychology (MP)
benefits of, 1, 42

defined, 174
goal of, 124
how it improves motivation, 88
methods of to deal with flawed
meanings, 99–100
as positing there are solutions to
human problems, 130
practitioner of, 174
role of/uses of, 6, 112
meaningful purpose, three pillars of, 44
meaningful settings
defined, 83
as element of meaningful meaning
ecology, 83*f*
meaningful state/experience, five
conditions of, 43, 48
The Meaningful Path, 43
meaning/important quadrant, 47*f*, 173
meaningless meaning accuracy,
122, 129
meaningless meaning exchange, 174
meaning-sclerosis, 95, 98, 173
meaning-sets
in action, 19–20
analysis of, 174
as compared to meaning-construct,
11–12
defined, 59, 173
dynamic nature of, 19
health of, 24
incomplete meaning-sets, 97
intelligence of, 27, 27–29*tt*
intrapersonal congruent meaning-
sets, 170
of personal, social and role
identities (PSRI), 58
relevance of, 36–38
role of, 9
strong and self-determined ones,
29–30, 30*t*
transactional meaning-set, 21

transformational meaning-set, 21
types of, 32
motivation
    as construct, 73
    defined, xxiv–xxv, 72–73, 75
    Energy/Motivational Intensity, 73*f*
    graphic of, 72*f*, 73*f*
    how MP improves, 88–89
    levels of, xxiv
    as one of six components of
        LIMA, 65
    as one of three components of
        identity, 55, 60, 61*f*, 64
    practitioner questions about,
        132–133
    and responsibility, 84
    role of, 61, 62
    triggers for, 84–85
    types of, 77*f*, 174
motivational intensity, 73*f*, 169
motives, xx, 4, 5, 7, 10, 18, 31, 73,
    84, 162
MP (meaningful purpose psychology).
    See meaningful purpose
    psychology (MP)
MTs (meaning types). *See* meaning
    types (MTs)
mutual, defined, 123
Myers, David G., 23, 92

N

natural attributes, 116–117, 174
Nehru, Jawaharlal, 109
Nevis, Sonia March, 16

O

obligatory social identity, 54, 55, 59*t*
other-oriented transformational
    meaning, 21, 22, 23
overconfidence bias, 21

P

The Path to a Meaningful Purpose
    (Marrero), xxi, 106
peace/peace of mind
    as Meaningful Life Striving, xxii,
        60, 83, 116, 122
    as one of five conditions of
        meaningful state/
        experience, 43
PERMA model, 43
person, social, and role identities
    (PSRI), 58, 59*t*, 175
person identity, 53, 104, 105–106,
    107, 175
practitioner questions
    about LIMA, 132–134
    and statements about meaning
        types (MTs), 135–136
prescribed worldview, as way to define
    default meaning of life, 109
preventative methods, defined, 175
projections, 95
prosperity
    as Meaningful Life Striving, xxii,
        60, 83, 116, 122
    as one of five conditions of
        meaningful state/
        experience, 43
PSRI (person, social, and role
    identities), 58, 59*t*, 175
psychological meaning DNA, 7,
    10, 175
psychophysiological phenomena, 95
purpose
    defined, 175
    as one of six components of
        LIMA, 65
    as one of three components of
        identity, 60, 61*f*, 64
    role of, 61, 62

purpose in action, practitioner
    questions about, 133

R

reasons, xx, 1, 3, 4, 5, 6, 7, 10, 17, 18,
    24, 31, 38, 39, 61, 154, 162
rebellious, as one of four possible
    reasons for demotivation, 75,
    81–82, 175
Reeve, John Marshall, 73
remedial support, 58, 175
repression, 93
resistance, 93
role identity, 57–58, 104, 107, 176
Ryan, Richard M., 42, 109, 113
Rychlack, Joseph F., 62, 85, 88–89

S

self-determined meaning of life, xxvi,
    35, 107, 111, 176
self-justification, 93
self-oriented transformational meaning,
    21, 22, 23
Situational Meaning-set (SMS), xxii, 9,
    31, 32, 33, 34, 176
social (group) identity, 54–57, 104–
    105, 107, 176
steered energy, 74, 75, 176
Stets, Jan E., 53, 104
strengths, defined, 117
strivings. *See* Five Life Strivings/Five
    Strivings

T

tactical retreat
    as one of four paths of energy,
        74, 83
    as type of motivation, 77*f*
talents, defined, 117
telosponse, 84–85, 85*f*, 86, 87*f*, 176
temporary groups, 56–57, 176

thelosponse, 86, 87*f*, 177
transactional meaning, 177
transcend, as T in ACT, xxii, 44, 50,
    60, 83, 90, 122, 156
transformational meaning, 21, 22, 177
true meaning, 2, 5
type-A personality, 77, 177

U

unimportant, important as contrasted
    with, 47, 47*f*, 48, 49

V

values
    congruent narratives and
        incongruent narratives of,
        125*f*
    examples of healthy and unhealthy
        ones, 25*t*
    intelligent and unintelligent
        descriptions and examples
        of, 28*t*
    as meaning type, xxii, 14–15
    practitioner questions and
        statements about, 136
    role of, 24
    sample questions to increase
        awareness of, 100
voluntary social identity, 56, 59*t*

W

Wilde, Oscar, 52
will
    as one of four paths of energy,
        74, 76
    as type of motivation, 77*f*
worldview
    defined, 94
    meanings as determining, 93, 121

End Notes

1. https://www.dictionary.com/browse/intention?s=t Accessed 16 December 2019.

2. Barbara L. Frederickson, *Positivity* (New York: Three Rivers Press, 2009), 183

3. https://www.dictionary.com/browse/misunderstanding?s=t Accessed 16 December 2019.

4. http://www.thefreedictionary.com/meaning Accessed 16 December 2019.

5. Alfred Adler, *What Life Should Mean to You* (Mansfield Centre, CT: Martino Publishing, 2010), 14

6. Joseph B. Fabry, *The Pursuit of Meaning: Viktor Frankl, Logotheray, and Life.* (Birmingham, Alabama: Purpose Research, LLC, 2013), xix

7. Alfred Adler, *What Life Could Mean to You.* (Center City, Minnesota: Hazelden, 1998), 1-2

8. Carol S. Dweck, *Self-Theories: Their Role in Motivation, Personality, and Development.* (Philadelphia: Psychology Press, 2000), xi

9. Joseph B. Fabry. *The Pursuit of Meaning: Viktor Frankl, Logotherapy, and Life* (Charlottesville: Purpose Research, LLC, 2013), xviii

10. Fabry, *"The Pursuit of Meaning"*, 96

11. Viktor E. Frankl, *Man's Search for Meaning* (Boston: Beacon Press, 2006), 145

12. Frankl, *"Man's Search for Meaning"*, 151

13. Roy F. Baumeister, *Meaning of Life* (New York: The Guilford Press, 1991), 6

14. Sonia March Nevis, *Gestalt Therapy: Perspectives and Applications,* (New York: Gardner Press, Inc., 1992), 69

15. Fabry, *"The Pursuit of Meaning"*, 40

16. Frankl, *"Man's Search for Meaning"*, 131

17. Frederickson, "Positivity", 161

18. E. Walster, E. Berscheid and G.W. Walster. "New directions in equity research." Journal of Personality and Social Psychology, 25 (1973): 1151-176. http://dx.doi.org/10.1037/h0033967

19. David G. Myers, *Social Psychology* (New York: McGraw-Hill, 2005), 460

20 https://authorluismarrero.blog/2017/11/28/building-a-meaningful-meaning-economy/ Accessed 16 December 2019

21 Intelligence-Wikipedia Accessed June 2, 2021

22 For those interested learning more about attribution, they are encouraged to study attribution theory, particularly the works of Fritz Heider, Harold Kelley, and Bernard Weiner.

23 Dweck, Carol S., *Mindset: The New Psychology of Success.* (New York: Ballantine Books, 2006)

24 Ibid

25 Gibb categories-Wikipedia. See also, Wilbers: Jack Gibb's Threatening vs. Supportive Communication Behaviors Accessed August 1, 2021

26 Luis A. Marrero, *The Path to a Meaningful Purpose: Psychological Foundations of Logoteleology* (Bloomington: IUniverse, 2013), 190-191

27 Dweck, Carol S. *Mindset: The New Psychology of Success.* (New York: Ballantine Books, 2006)

28 https://www.thefreedictionary.com/introjection Accessed 16 December 2019.

29 61 Best Quotes And Sayings About Character (askideas.com) Accessed April 9, 2021

30 Richard M. Ryan, Kennon M. Sheldon, Tim Kasser, and Edward L. Deci, "All Goals Are Not Created Equal: An Organistic Perspective of Goals and Regulation" in *The Psychology of Action: Linking Cognition and Motivation to Behavior,* Peter M. Gollwitzer, and John A. Bargh, eds. *(New York: The Guilford Press, 1996),* 13

31 The PERMA Model: Your Scientific Theory of Happiness (positivepsychology. com) Accessed August 2, 2021.

32 The Philosophy of Ikigai: 3 Examples About Finding Purpose (positivepsychology. com) Accessed August 2, 2021.

33 MacGregor Burns, James, *Leadership.* (New York: Harper & Row Publishers, 1978), 79

34 Are You "Other-Oriented"? | Psychology Today Accessed August 2, 2021. See also, Grant, Adam, *Give and Take* (New York: Penguin Books, 2013)

35 https://www.dictionary.com/browse/meaningless?s=t Accessed 16 December 2019.

36 Harold F. Pashler, *The Psychology of Attention.* (Cambridge, Massachusetts: The MIT Press, 1998), 14

37 https://binged.it/2PQGeeb Accessed 8 April 2021

38 Peter J. Burke, and Jan E. Stets, *Identity Theory.* (New York: Oxford University Press, 2009)

39 Ibid, 112

40 Based on Burke, Peter J., and Stets, Jan E., *Identity Theory*. (New York: Oxford University Press, 2009)

41 Dorothée Legrand, "Bodily Intention and the Unreasonable Intentional Agent," in *Naturalizing Intention in Action,* eds. Franck Grammont, Dorothée Legrand, and Pierre Livet, (Cambridge, MA: Massachusetts Institute of Technology, 2010), 166

42 Joseph F. Rychlack, *Logical Learning Theory: A Human Teleology and Its Empirical Support* (Lincoln: University of Nebraska Press, 1994), 37

43 Frankl, *"Man's Search for Meaning",* 99

44 Frankl, Viktor, *Psychotherapy and Existentialism,* (New York: Pocket Books, 1967), 38

45 JohnMarshall Reeve, *Understanding Motivation and Emotion,* 4th ed. (Hoboken, NJ: John Wiley & Sons, Inc., 2005), 6

46 Richard M. Ryan, Kennon M. Sheldon, Tim Kasser, and Edward L. Deci, "All Goas Are Not Created Equal: An Organistic Perspective of Goals and Regulation" in *The Psychology of Action,* 7-26. See also, Icek Ajzen, "The Directive Influence of Attitudes in Behavior" in *The Psychology of Action,* 385-403

47 Azjen, "The Directive Influence of Attitudes in Behavior", 400

48 Self-Transcendence as a Human Phenomenon (blogotherapy.co.il), 100

49 https://www.yourdictionary.com/activity-trap Accessed 13 April 2021

50 Arthur Reber, Rhiannon Allen & Emily S. Reber, *The Penguin Dictionary of Psychology* (New York: Penguin Reference Library, 2009) 840

51 https://www.harleytherapy.co.uk/counselling/dependent-personality-disorder.htm Accessed 16 December 2019.

52 We propose reading, Passmore Oades (2014). Positive Psychology Active Constructive Responding.pdf (reading.ac.uk) and Active-Constructive-Responding.pdf (positivepsychology.com), based on gable et al. 2004.pdf (ucsb.edu) Accessed 3 September 2021

53 Mihaly Csikszentmihalyi, *Flow: the psychology of optimal experience* (New York: HarperCollins Publishers, 1990), 4

54 Rychlack, *Logical Learning Theory:* 36

55 Rychlack, "Logical Learning Theory", 36

56 Frederickson, *"Positivity",* 49

57 Rychlack, "Logical Learning Theory", 106

58 Quote by Albert Einstein: "Any fool can know. The point is to understand." (goodreads.com) Accessed 15 April 2021

59 David G. Myers, *Social Psychology,* 8th ed. (New York: McGraw-Hill, 2005), 96

60 60 https://www.bing.com/search?q=what+is+a+worldview&FORM=QSRE6 Accessed 4 January 2020.

61 https://www.dictionary.com/browse/calcification Accessed 16 December 2019.

62 Pashler, Harold E., *The Psychology of Attention* (Cambridge, Massachusetts: MIT Press, 1999), 37-165

63 https://authorluismarrero.blog/2017/07/17/what-makes-a-meaning-a-logoteleological-perspective/ Accessed 16 December 2019.

64 https://authorluismarrero.blog/2017/12/19/blocks-to-meaning-the-calcification-of-awareness/ Accessed 16 December 2019.

65 Robert L. Leahy, *Overcoming Resistance in Cognitive Therapy* (New York: The Guilford Press, 2001); Robert J. Marshak, *Covert Processes at Work* (San Francisco: Berrett-Koehler Publishers, Inc., 2006); Cheri Huber and Ashwini Narayanan, *I Don't Want to, I Don't Feel Like It* (United States of America: Keep It Simple Books, 2013); Eric Berne, *A Layman's Guide to Psychiatry and Psychoanalysis* (New York: Ballantine Books: 1976); Vohs, Kathleen D. Vohs and Roy F. Baumeister, eds. *Handbook of Self-Regulation: Research, Theory, and Applications* (New York: The Guilford Press, 2011)

66 www.wisesayings.com/authors/alfred-adler-quotes/?sm=61079#61079 Accessed October 14, 2021

67 www.wisesayings.com/authors/alfred-adler-quotes/?sm=16484#16484 Accessed October 14, 2021

68 Quote by Alfred Adler: "A lie would have no sense unless the truth were..." (goodreads.com) Accessed October 14, 2021

69 Frederickson, "Positivity", 171

70 Alfred Adler Quotes and Sayings | Wise Sayings Accessed October 14, 2021

71 Gabriel García Márquez, *Love in the Time of Cholera,* trans. Edith Grossman (New York: Vintage Books, 1988), 165

72 Peter J. Burke, and Jan E. Stets, *Identity Theory* (New York: Oxford University Press, 2009)

73 Ibid. page 114

74 Ibid. page 118

75 Ibid. page 124

76 Luis A. Marrero, *The Path to a Meaningful Purpose: Psychological Foundations of Logoteleology* (Bloomington: IUniverse LLC, 2013), 75

77 Ibid. page 31

78 Jawaharlal Nehru-Life is like a game of cards. The hand... (brainyquote.com) Accessed 15 April 2021

79 Claude M. Steiner, *Scripts People Live* (New York: Bantam Psychology Books, 1975), 82-83

80 https://www.thefreedictionary.com/introjection Accessed 16 December 2019.

81   Richard M. Ryan, Kennon M. Sheldom, Tim Kasser, and Edward L. Deci "All Goals Are Not Created Equal." Gollowitzer, Peter M., and John A. Bargh, eds. in *The Psychology of Action: Linking Cognition and Motivation to Behavior* (New York: The Guilford Press, 1996) 11

82   Heinz L. Ansbacher, and Rowena R. Ansbacher, eds, *The Individual Psychology of Alfred Adler, 1ˢᵗ ed.* (New York: Basic Books, 1956), 89

83   Edward L. Deci, and Richard M. Ryan, "1: Overview of Self-Determination Theory: An Organismic Dialectical Perspective", in *Handbook of Self-Determination Research,* eds. Edward L. Deci, and Richard M. Ryan *(*New York: The University of Rochester Press, 2002), 3

84   In logoteleology, the meaning of life is based on identity theories, while meaning in life is based on motivation and self-determination theories.

85   Csikszentmihalyi, *"Flow",* 4

86   Please refer to the content of "Chapter 2: What is Meaningful and Important?" Marrero, Luis A. *The Path to a Meaningful Purpose. 2013*

87   Ibid

88   www.brainyquote.com

89   https://authorluismarrero.blog/2016/08/09/meaning-meaningful-and-important-the-powerful-three/ Accessed 16 December 2019.

90   https://www.merriam-webster.com/dictionary/accuracy Accessed 16 December 2019.

91   https://binged.it/2kozLri Accessed 16 December 2019.

92   https://binged.it/2lWnJ9b Accessed 16 December 2019.

93   William Ikes, "Introduction." William Ikes, Ed. *Compatible and Incompatible Relationships (*New York: Springer-Verlag, 1985), 1

94   https://www.merriam-webster.com/dictionary/congruence Accessed 16 December 2019.

95   https://authorluismarrero.blog/2017/12/19/blocks-to-meaning-the-calcification-of-awareness/ Accessed 16 December 2019.

96   https://authorluismarrero.blog/2016/08/09/meaning-meaningful-and-important-the-powerful-three/ Accessed 16 December 2019.

Bibliography / Suggested Reading

Adler, Alfred. *What Life Could Mean to You.* Center City, MN: Hazeldn, 1998.

Adler, A. *What Life Should Mean to You.* CT: Martino, 2010.

Anda, R., et al. "Depressed Affect, Hopelessness, and the Risk of Ischemic Heart Disease in a Cohort of US Adults." Epidemiology 4 (1993).

Ansbacher, Heinz L., and Rowena R. Ansbacher, Eds. *The Individual Psychology of Alfred Adler.* New York: Harper and Row, 1956.

Arnold, M. B. *Emotion and Personality* (Vols. 1 and 2). New York: Columbia University Press, 1960.

Arnold, M. B. "Perennial Problems in the Field of Emotion." *Feelings and Emotions.* New York: Academic Press (1970), 169–85.

Baard, Paul. "Intrinsic Need Satisfaction in Organizations: A Motivational Basis for Success in For-Profit and Not-For-Profit Settings." 2002.

Bains, G., et al. *Meaning Inc.* Glasgow: Profile Books, 2007.

Bandura, A. "Self-Referent Thought: A Developmental Analysis of Self-Efficacy." *Social Cognitive Development: Frontiers and Possible Futures.* Cambridge, UK: Cambridge University Press, 1981. 200–239.

Baumeister, Roy F. "Self-Regulation and Ego Threat: Motivated Cognition, Self-Deception, and Destructive Goal Setting." Gollwitzer, Peter M., and John

A. Bargh, Eds. *The Psychology of Action: Linking Cognition and Motivation to Behavior.* New York: The Guilford Press, 1996. 27-47

Baumeister, R., and M. R. Leary. "The Need to Belong: Desire for Interpersonal Attachments as a Fundamental Human Motivation." *Psychological Bulletin* 117 (1995): 479–529.

Berne, Eric. *A Layman's Guide to Psychiatry and Psychoanalysis.* New York: Ballantine Books: 1976.

Blacksmith, N., and J. Harter. October 28, 2011. "Majority of American Workers Not Engaged in Their Jobs." http://www.gallup.com/ poll/150383/majority-american-workers-not-engaged-jobs.aspx.

Bogdan, Radu J. *Grounds for Cognition: How Goal-Guided Behavior Shapes the Mind.* Hillsdale, NJ: Lawrence Erlbaum Associates, Inc. Publishers, 1994.

Bowlby, John. *Loss, Sadness, and Depression.* Vol. III of Attachment and Loss. London: Basic Books, 1980.

Burke, Peter J., and Jan E. Stets. *Identity Theory.* New York: Oxford University Press, 2009.

Carton, J. S., and S. Nowicki. "Antecedents of Individual Differences in Locus of Control of Reinforcement: A Critical Review." *Genetic, Social, and General Psychology Monographs* 120: (1994)31–81.

Csikszentmihalyi, Mihaly. *Flow.* New York: Harper Perennial Modern Classics, 1990.

Cohen, I. S., Ed. "The G. Stanley Hall Lecture Series (Vol. 9, 39–73). Washington, DC: American Psychological Association.

Cohen, S., D. R. Sherrod, and M. S. Clark. "Social Skills and the Stress-Protective Role of Social Support." *Journal of Personality and Social Psychology* 50 (1986): 963–973.

Coles, Robert, ed. *The Eric Erikson Reader*, New York: W. W. Norton Company, Inc., 2000.

Compton, William C. and Edward Hoffman. *Positive Psychology: The Science of Happiness and Flourishing.* (2nd edition). Belmont, CA: Wadsworth, 2013

Costa, P. T., and R. R. McCrae. "Influence of Extraversion and Neuroticism on Subjective Well-Being: Happy and Unhappy People." *Journal of Personality and Social Psychology* 38 (1980): 668–78.

Costello, Stephen J. "An Existential Analysis of Anxiety: Frankl, Kierkegaard, Voegelin." *Journal of Search for Meaning* 34, no. 2.

Davidson, R. J. "On Emotion, Mood, and Related Affective Constructs." Ekman, P., and R. J. Davidson, Eds., *The Nature of Emotion: Fundamental Questions.* New York: Oxford University Press, 1994. 51–55.

Davis, C. G., S. Nolen-Hoeksema, and J. Larsen. "Making Sense of Loss and Benefiting from the Experience: Two Construals of Meaning." Journal of Personality and Social Psychology 75 (1998): 561–74.

Deci, E. L., and R. M. Ryan. "The Support of Autonomy and the Control of Behavior." *Journal of Personality and Social Psychology* 53 (1987): 1024–37.

Deci, E. L., and R. M. Ryan. *Intrinsic Motivation and Self-Determination in Human Behavior.* New York: Plenum, 1985.

Deci, E. L., and R. M. Ryan, Eds. *Handbook of Self-Determination Research.* New York: The University of Rochester Press, 2002.

Depue, R. A., and P. F. Collins. "Neurobiology of the Structure of Personality: Dopamine Facilitation of Incentive Motivation and Extraversion." *Behavioral and Brain Sciences* 22 (1999): 491–569.

Diener, E., E. Sandvik, W. Pavot, and F. Fujita. "Extraversion and Subjective Well-Being in a US National Probability Sample." *Journal of Research in Personality* 26 (1998): 205–15.

Dweck, Carol S. Self-Theories: *Their Role in Motivation, Personality, and Development*. Philadelphia: Psychology Press, 2000.

Dweck, Carol S. *Mindset: The New Psychology of Success*. New York: Ballantine Books, 2006

Dykman, B. M. "Integrating Cognitive and Motivational Factors in Depression: Initial Tests of a Goal-Orientation Approach." *Journal of Personality and Social Psychology* 74 (1998): 139–58.

Ekman, P. "All Emotions Are Basic." Ekman, P., and R. J. Davidson, Eds. *The Nature of Emotion: Fundamental Questions*. New York: Oxford University Press, 1994. 15–19.

Elliot, A. J., and T. M. Trash. "Approach-Avoidance Motivation in Personality: Approach and Avoidance Temperament and Goals." *Journal of Personality and Social Psychology* 82 (2002): 804–18.

Erikson, E. *The Life Cycle Completed*. New York: W. W. Norton and Company, 1997.

Fabry, Joseph B. *The Pursuit of Meaning: Viktor Frankl, Logotherapy, and Life*. Charlottesville: Purpose Research, LLC., 2013.

Feldman, D.B., and C.R. Snyder. "Hope and the Meaningful Life: Theoretical and Empirical Associations between Goal-Directed Thinking and Life Meaning." *Journal of Social and Clinical Psychology* 24, no. 3 (2005): 401–21.

Findley, M. J., and H. M. Cooper. "Locus of Control and Academic Achievement: A Literature Review." *Journal of Personality and Social Psychology* 44 (1983): 419–27.

Frankl, Viktor E., *Man's Search for Meaning*. Boston: Beacon Press, 2006.

Frankl, Viktor E. *The Will to Meaning: Foundations and Applications of Logotherapy*. New York: Meridian, 1998.

Frankl, V. E. *Man's Search for Ultimate Meaning*. New York, NY: Basic Books, 2000.

Frankl, Viktor, *Man's Search for Ultimate Meaning*. Boston: Beacon Press, 2006.

Frankl, Viktor. *Psychoanalysis and Existentialism*. New York: Pocket Books, 1967.

Frankl, Viktor E., *The Doctor and the Soul: From Psychotherapy to Logotherapy*. New York: Vintage Books, 1983.

Frankl, Viktor E., *The Unheard Cry for Meaning*. New York: Touchstone, 1978.

Frankl, Viktor E., *The Will to Meaning*. New York: Meridian, 1988.

Freasure-Smith, et al., "Gender, Depression, and One-Year Prognosis after Myocardial Infarction." *Psychosomatic Medicine* 61 (1999): 26–37.

Frederciskson, Barbara L., *Positivity*. New York: Three Rivers Press, 2009.

Granit, Ragnar. *The Purposive Brain*. Cambridge, MA, and London, England: The MIT Press, 1981.

Gunnar, M. R. "Contingent Stimulation: A Review of Its Role in Early Development." Levine, S., and H. Ursin, Eds. *Coping and Health*. New York: Plenum, 1980. 101–19.

Heckhausen, H., *Motivation and Handeln*. New York: Springer-Verlag, 1980.

Hogg, Michael A., "Social Identity Theory." *Contemporary Social Psychological Theories*. Burke, P. J., Ed. Stanford: Stanford University Press, 2006. 111–36.

Huber, Cheri and Ashwini Narayanan, *I Don't Want to, I Don't Feel Like It*. United States of America: Keep It Simple Books, 2013.

Huckabay, Mary Ann, "An Overview of the Theory and Practice of Gestalt Group Process." Nevis, Edwin C., Ed. *Gestalt Therapy: Perspective and Applications*. New York: Gardner Press, Inc. 1992.

Ikes, William. "Introduction." Ikes, William, Editor. *Compatible and Incompatible Relationships*. New York: Springer-Verlag, 1985. 1

Inamori, Kazuo, *For People and for Profit*. Tokyo: Kodansha International Ltd, 1997.

Izard, C. E., "The Structure and Functions of Emotions: Implications for Cognition, Motivation, and Personality." *The G. Stanley Hall Lecture Series* (Vol. 9, 39–73). Washington, DC: American Psychological Association, 1989.

Izard, C. E., and C. Z. Malatesta, "Perspectives in Emotional Development: I. Differential Emotions Theory or Early Emotional Development." *Handbook of Infant Development* (2nd ed., 494–554). New York: Wiley-Interscience, 1987.

Izard, C. E., *The Psychology of Emotions*. New York: Plenum, 1991.

Izard, C. E., "Basic Emotions, Relations among Emotions, and Emotion-Cognition Relations." *Psychological Review* 99 (1992): 561–65.

Izard, C. E., "Four Systems for Emotion Activation: Cognitive and Noncognitive Development." *Psychological Review* 100 (1993):68–90

Janis, Irving L., *Victims of Groupthink*. New York: Houghton Mifflin, 1972.

Jung, Carl. Summary. n.d. http://www.sonoma.edu/users/d/daniels/Jungsum.html. Retrieved October 13, 2020.

Kasser, T., "Two Versions of the American Dream: Which Goals and Values Make for a High Quality of Life?" Diener, E., and D. Rahtz, Eds. *Advances in Quality of Life: Theory and Research*. Dordrecht, Netherlands: Kluwer, 2000.

Kasser, T., *The High Price of Materialism*. Cambridge, MA: MIT Press, 2002.

Kegan, Robert, and Lisa Laskow Lahey, *Immunity to Change*. Boston: Harvard Business Press, 2009

Koestner, Richard, and Gaëtan F. Losier, "Distinguishing Three Ways of Being Internally Motivated: A Closer Look at Introjection, Identification, and Intrinsic Motivation.", 2002.

Kresge, Elijah Everett, *Kant's Doctrine of Teleology*. Allentown, PA: The Francis Printing Company, 1914.

Leahy, Robert L., *Overcoming Resistance in Cognitive Therapy*. New York: The Guilford Press, 2001.

Lefcourt, H. M., *Locus of Control: Current Trends in Theory and Research*. Hillsdale, NJ: Erlbaum, 1982.

Lepore, S. J., "Social Conflict, Social Support, and Psychological Distress: Evidence of Cross-Domain Buffering Effects." Journal of Personality and Social Psychology 63 (1992): 857–67.

Lewin, Kurt, *A Dynamic Theory of Personality: Selected Papers*. Adams, D. E., and K. E. Zener, Trans. New York: McGraw Hill, 1935.

Lewin, K., "Action Research and Minority Problems." *Journal of Social Issues* 2, no. 4 (1946): 34–36.

Lucas, R. E., and F. Fujita, "Factors Influencing the Relation between Extraversion and Pleasant Affect." *Journal of Personality and Social Psychology* 79 (2000): 1039–56.

Maio, Gregory R., and Geoffrey Haddock. *The Psychology of Attitudes and Attitude Change*. Los Angeles: Sage, 2009.

Maddux, J. E., and J. T. Gosselin, "Self-Efficacy." Leary, M. R., and J. P. Tangney, Eds. *Handbook of Self and Identity*. New York: Guilford, 2003.

Markus, H., and E. Wurf, "The Dynamic Self-Concept: A Social Psychological Perspective." *Annual Review of Psychology* 38 (1987): 299–337.

Marrero, Luis A. *The Path to a Meaningful Purpose: Psychological Foundations of Logoteleology.* Bloomington: IUniverse, 2013.

Marshak, Robert J., *Covert Processes at Work.* San Francisco: Berrett-Koehler Publishers, Inc., 2006.

Mathers, Dale. *Meaning and Purpose in Analytical Psychology.* Philadelphia: Taylor and Francis Inc, 2001.

McAdams, D. P., "A Thematic Coding System for the Intimacy Motive." *Journal of Research in Personality* 14 (1980): 413–32.

Medin, Douglas L., and Brian H. Ross, *Cognitive Psychology.* Orlando, FL: Harcourt Brace and Company, 1997.

Medin, Douglas L., and Brian H. Ross, *Cognitive Psychology.* Fort Worth, TX: Harcourt Brace College Publishers, 1996.

Miller, Frederic P., Agnes F. Vandome, and John McBrewster, Eds., *Four Causes.* Lexington, KY: Alphascript Publishing, 2009.

Miller, K. I., and P. R. Monge, "Participation, Satisfaction, and Productivity: A Meta-Analytic Review." *Academy of Management Journal* 29 (1986): 727–53.

Mourkogiannis, Nikos, *Purpose: The Starting Point of Great Companies.* New York: Palgrave Macmillan, 2006.

Myers, D. G., *Social Psychology.* New York, NY: McGraw-Hill, 2005. Nevis, Edwin C., Ed., Gestalt Therapy. New York: Gardner Press, 1992.

Novellino, Michele, "On Closer Analysis: Unconscious Communication in the Adult Ego State and a Revision of the Rules of Communication within the Framework of Transactional Psychoanalysis." New York: Grove Press, 2003.

Osgood, C. E., *An Alternative to War or Surrender.* Urbana, IL: University of Illinois Press, 1962.

Osgood, C. E., "GRIT: A Strategy for Survival in Mankind's Nuclear Age?" Paper Presented at the Pugwash Conference on New Directions in Disarmament, Racine, WI, 1980.

Pashler, Harold F., *The Psychology of Attention*. Cambridge, Massachusetts: The MIT Press, 1998.

Park, C. L., and S. Folkman, "Meaning in the Context of Stress and Coping." *Review of General Psychology* 1 (1997): 115–44.

Pederson, N. C., et al., "Neuroticism, Extraversion, and Related Traits in Adult Twins Reared Apart and Reared Together." *Journal of Personality and Social Psychology* 55 (1988): 950–57.

Pierce, G. R., B. R. Sarason, and I. G. Sarason, "General and Relationship-Based Perceptions of Social Support: Are Two Constructs Better Than One?" *Journal of Personality and Social Psychology* 61 (1991): 1028–39.

Pierce, G. R., B. R. Sarason, and I. G. Sarason, Eds., *Handbook of Social Support and the Family*. New York: Plenum Press, 1996.

Purpose (n.d.). http://www.macmillandictionary.com/dictionary/ american/ purpose. Retrieved October 13, 2020.

Reber, Arthur, Rhiannon Allen & Emily S. Reber, *The Penguin Dictionary of Psychology* (New York: Penguin Reference Library, 2009) 840

Reber, Arthur S., Rhianon Allen, and Emily S. Reber, *Penguin Dictionary of Psychology*. New York: Penguin Books, 2009.

Reeve, Johnmarshall. *Understanding Motivation and Emotion*. New Jersey: John Wiley and Sons, Inc., 2005.

Reeve, Johnmarshall. "Self-Determination Theory Applied to Educational Settings." Eds. Edward L. Deci and Richard M. Ryan. *Handbook of Self-Determination Research*. Rochester: The University of Rochester Press, 2002.

Reis, H. T., and P. Franks, "The Role of Intimacy and Social Support in Health Outcomes: Two Processes Or One?" *Personal Relationships* 1 (1994): 185–97.

Rogers, Carl. *On Becoming a Person: A Therapist's View of Psychotherapy.* Boston: Houghton Mifflin Company, 1989.

Ruvolo, A., and H. Markus. "Possible Selves and Performance: The Power of Self-Relevant Imagery." *Social Cognition* 9 (1992): 95–124.

Ryan, Richard M., et al., "All Goals Are Not Created Equal: An Organistic Perspective of Goals and Regulation." *The Psychology of Action: Linking Cognition and Motivation to Behavior.* New York: The Guilford Press, 1996. 7–26.

Ryan, Richard M., et al., Eds., "Overview of Self-Determination Theory: An Organismic Dialectical Perspective." Ryan, Richard M., and Edward L. Deci, Eds. *Handbook of Self-Determination Research.* Rochester: The University of Rochester Press, 2002.

Ryan, R. M., "Psychological Needs and the Facilitation of Integrative Processes." *Journal of Personality* 63 (1995): 397–427.

Rychlack, Joseph F., *Logical Learning Theory: A Human Teleology and Its Empirical Support.* Lincoln: University of Nebraska Press, 1994.

Sarason, B. R., et al., "Perceived Social Support and Working Models of Self and Actual Others." *Journal of Personality and Social Psychology* 60 (1991): 273–87.

Schneewind, K. A.,"Impact of Family Processes on Control Beliefs." Bandura, A., Ed. *Self-Efficacy in Changing Societies.* New York: Cambridge University Press, 1995. 114–48.

Schultz, D.P., and S. E. Schultz, *A History of Modern Psychology.* Belmont, CA: Wadsworth, Cengage Learning, 2012.

Seligman, Martin E. P., *Flourish.* New York: Free Press, 2011.

Senge, Peter, et al., *Presence: Human Purpose and the Field of the Future*. New York: Currency, 2004.

Sills, Charlotte, and Helena Hargaden, Eds. *Ego States: Key Concepts in Transactional Analysis: Contemporary Views*. London, UK: Worth Publishing.

Sisodia, Rajendr S., David B. Wolfe, and Jagdish N. Sheth, *Firms of Endearment*. New Jersey: Wharton School Publishing, 2007.

Skinner, Ellen, and Kath Edge, "Self-Determination, Coping, and Development," *Handbook of Self-Determination Research*. New York: The University of Rochester Press, 2002.

Skinner, E. A., J. Zimmer-Gembeck, and J. P. Connell, "Individual Differences and Development of Perceived Control." *Monographs of the Society for Research in Child Development*, whole no. 204, 1998.

Stets, Jan E., and Peter J. Burke. Sociological Perspectives 38: 129–50. 1994. And "Inconsistent Self-Views in the Control Identity Model." *Social Science Research* 23: 236–62.

Steger, Michael F., and Joo Yeon Shin, "The Relevance of Meaning in Life Questionnaire to Therapeutic Practice: A Look at the Initial Evidence." The International Forum of Logotherapy: *Journal of Search for Meaning* 33, no. 2 (2010): 95–104.

Steiner, Claude, *Scripts People Live*. New York: Grover Press, 1974.

Stets, Jan E., and Peter J. Burke, "Identity Theory and Social Identity Theory." *Social Psychology Quarterly* 63 (2000): 224–37.

Swan, W. B., and S. J. Read, "Self-Verification Processes: How We Sustain Our Self-Conceptions." *Journal of Experimental Psychology* 17 (1981): 351–72.

Swan, W. B., and S. J. Read, "Acquiring Self-Knowledge: The Search for Feedback That Fits." *Journal of Personality and Social Psychology* 41 (1981): 1119–28.

Swann, W. B. Jr., "Self-Verification Theory." Van Lang, P., A. Kruglanski, and E. T. Higgins, Eds. *Handbook of Theories of Social Psychology*. London (2012): Sage, 23–42.

Tangney, J. P., R. F. Bauemeister, and A. L. Boone, "High Self-Control Predicts Good Adjustment, Less Pathology, Better Grades, and Interpersonal Success." *Journal of Personality* 72 (2004): 271–324.

Taylor, S. E., "Adjustment to Threatening Events: A Theory of Cognitive Adaptation." *American Psychologist* 38 (1983): 1161–73.

Tesser, A., L. Martin, and D. Cornell, "On the Substitutability of Self-Protective Mechanisms." *The Psychology of Action*. New York: Guilford Press, 1996. 51.

Thoits, Peggy A., "Multiple Identities and Psychological Well-Being: A Reformulation and Test of the Social Isolation Hypothesis." *American Sociological Review* 49: 174–87. Also: 1986. "Multiple Identities: Examining Gender and Marital Status Differences in Distress." *American Sociological Review* 51 (1983): 259–72.

Vallerand, Robert J., and Catherine F. Ratelle, "Intrinsic and Extrinsic Motivation: A Hierarchical Model.", 2002.

Vohs, Kathleen D. and Roy F. Baumeister, eds. *Handbook of Self-Regulation: Research, Theory, and Applications*. New York: The Guilford Press, 2011.

Vos, Joel. *Meaning in Life*. London, UK: Palgrave, 2018

Walster, E., Berscheid, E., & Walster, G.W. (1973). New directions in equity research. *Journal of Personality and Social Psychology, 25,* 1151-176.

Watson D., and L. A. Clark, "Extraversion and Its Positive Emotional Core." *Handbook of Personality Psychology*. San Diego, CA: Academic Press, 1997. 767–93.

Whitney, M. October 2, 2009. "Exclusive: New Poll Shows Clear Majorities Distrust Big Corporations, Favor Unions." http:// workinprogress.firedoglake.

com/2009/10/02/exclusive-new-poll-shows-clear-majorities-distrust-big-corporations-favor-unions/.

Weir, Michael, *Goal-Directed Behavior*. New York: Gordon and Breach Science Publishers, 1984.

Zajonc, R. B. "Feeling and Thinking: Preferences Need No Inferences." *American Psychologist* 35 (1980): 159.

Zajonc, Robert B., "Social Facilitation." *Science* 149 (1965): 296–274.

Printed in the United States
by Baker & Taylor Publisher Services